Relics *of the* Christ

RELICS

OF THE

CHRIST

Joe Nickell

THE UNIVERSITY PRESS OF KENTUCKY

Publication of this volume was made possible in part
by a grant from the National Endowment for the Humanities.

Scholarly publisher for the Commonwealth,
serving Bellarmine University, Berea College, Centre
College of Kentucky, Eastern Kentucky University,
The Filson Historical Society, Georgetown College,
Kentucky Historical Society, Kentucky State University,
Morehead State University, Murray State University,
Northern Kentucky University, Transylvania University,
University of Kentucky, University of Louisville,
and Western Kentucky University.

Editorial and Sales Offices: The University Press of Kentucky
663 South Limestone Street, Lexington, Kentucky 40508-4008
www.kentuckypress.com

11 10 09 08 07   5 4 3 2 1

Library of Congress Cataloging-in-Publication Data
Nickell, Joe.
  Relics of the Christ / Joe Nickell.
     p. cm.
  Includes bibliographical references and index.
  ISBN-13: 978-0-8131-2425-4 (hardcover : alk. paper)
  ISBN-10: 0-8131-2425-5 (hardcover : alk. paper)
  1. Jesus Christ—Relics. 2. Relics. 3. Religious articles. I. Title.
  BT465.N53 2006
  232.96'6—dc22

                              2006029341

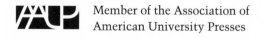 Member of the Association of
American University Presses

Contents

Illustrations

Acknowledgments

I am grateful for the assistance of many people, including all my colleagues at the Center for Inquiry in Amherst, New York, notably, Paul Kurtz, chairman, and Barry Karr, executive director, for their continued support. So, too, the entire staff of *Skeptical Inquirer* magazine, in which some portions of this book appeared.

Specifically, I want to thank Timothy Binga, director of CFI Libraries, for research assistance; Thomas Flynn, editor of *Free Inquiry*, for help in various ways; and Paul E. Loynes for word processing.

I appreciate all the efforts of the staff at the University Press of Kentucky, especially Gena Henry for her continuing interest in this book.

Many others assisted in various ways, especially my Italian colleagues and friends, including Paola de Gobbi, Francesco Chiminello, and Matteo Fillippini (in Venice); Massimo Polidoro (in Milan); Stefano Bagnasco, Andrea Ferrero, Claudio Pastore, Beatrice Mautino, and Mario Tomatis (in Turin); and Luigi Garlaschelli (who accompanied me to Naples).

And, of course, once again I am grateful for the encouragement and assistance of friends and family, especially the love of my life, Diana Harris; our beautiful daughter, Cherette Roycroft; my son-in-law, Randy Roycroft; and my grandsons, Chase and Tyner.

The Life of Jesus

The founder of Christianity, the religious movement that helped shape the course of Western civilization, was an itinerant, wonder-working, Palestinian rabbi from Nazareth named Yeshua (in Hebrew), today known as Jesus (from the Greek form of that name). He has been viewed in quite different ways. As portrayed in the Christian Gospels, he was the Messiah, or Christ (from the Greek "anointed"); scholars have attempted to understand him as a historical figure, sometimes called the Nazarene; and some have even seen him as largely or even completely fictitious, the product of an evolving mythology. This chapter treats each of these views in turn and then sets the tone for the remainder of the book, which investigates the reputed relics of Jesus and his family and followers, examining how they contribute to an understanding of what is necessarily a story of a story.

The Christ

The primary source of information about the life of Jesus is the four Gospels—Matthew, Mark, Luke, and John—supplemented by other Christian texts, including apocryphal Gospels, and scant non-Christian writings. Three of the four Gospels—Matthew, Mark, and Luke—are known as the synoptic Gospels (from the Greek *synoptikos*, "with one eye") because of their similarities. Matthew appears first in the canon, although it is now believed that Mark was written earlier (Asimov 1969, 108). Matthew addresses a Jewish audience, Luke a largely Gentile one, and both appear to have used Mark as a source, possibly in an earlier form. John's Gospel "is an independent production, reporting sayings of Jesus in the form of discourses that differ from the accounts of the other three" (*Encyclopaedia Britannica* 1960, s.v. "Jesus Christ").

Mark's Gospel says almost nothing about the origins of Jesus. Matthew (1:1–16) and Luke (3:23–38) provide genealogies, but they are contradictory as to the father of Joseph, Jesus' father, "as was supposed" (Luke 3:23). Luke's questioning of the identity of Jesus' father may acknowledge the evangelist's acceptance of the virgin birth, or it might be an early scribe's insertion (Asimov 1969, 275). The forthcoming birth was announced by an angel that appeared to either Joseph (Matthew 1:20–24) or Mary (Luke 1:26–38); see figure I.1. Only Matthew (2:1–3) tells of "wise men" (Magi) from the east who are led by a star to "worship" Jesus, born in Bethlehem, as "King of the Jews." Only Luke (2:8–18) relates how an angel told shepherds of the birth, prompting them to visit the manger where the infant lay, there having been "no room . . . in the inn."

Again, only Luke (2:40–50) tells the story of twelve-year-old Jesus visiting the temple in Jerusalem and astonishing his elders with his brilliance. Luke (2:52) then skips over the early years by stating, "And Jesus increased in wisdom and stature, and in favour with God and man." Next, all four Gospels relate Jesus' baptism by John the Baptist, a historical figure mentioned by Josephus. In Mark (1:9–11), the Spirit of God enters Jesus on this occasion; in Matthew (3:14–15), however, the Holy Spirit had already entered Jesus when he was conceived, so the focus is on John the Baptist recognizing that Jesus is the Messiah.

Following a period of fasting and soul-searching—dramatized by Matthew (4:1–11) as a series of temptations by the devil—Jesus begins his ministry of teaching and working miracles. Rejected by his fellow Nazarenes for daring to compare himself with the prophets

Figure I.1. The Annunciation of Jesus' birth is related in the Gospel of Luke (mid-nineteenth-century illustration by Julius Schnorr von Carolsfeld).

Elijah and Elisha, he states: "A prophet is not without honour, but in his own country, and among his own kin, and in his own house" (Mark 6:4). He proceeds to nearby Galilee, and, writes Matthew (4:17), "From that time Jesus began to preach, and to say, 'Repent: for the kingdom of heaven is at hand.'" At the shore of the Lake of Gennesaret (later known as the Sea of Galilee), Jesus sees two fishermen, Simon Peter and his brother Andrew, casting a net, and he says, "Follow me, and I will make you fishers of men" (Matthew 4:19).

The multitudes begin to gather and to follow him, and he delivers what came to be known as the Sermon on the Mount. This is actually less a sermon than a collection of representative sayings, which typically express Old Testament teachings (Asimov 1969,

165). For example, Jesus says, "Blessed are the meek: for they shall inherit the earth" (Matthew 5:5); this follows Psalms 37:11, "But the meek shall inherit the earth."

Jesus often taught through parables, such as that of the sower:

> Behold a sower went forth to sow. And when he sowed, some seeds fell by the way side, and the fowls came and devoured them up: Some fell upon stony places, where they had not much earth: and forthwith they sprung up, because they had no deepness of earth: And when the sun was up they were scorched; and because they had no root, they withered away. And some fell among thorns; and the thorns sprung up, and choked them: But other fell into good ground, and brought forth fruit, some an hundredfold, some sixtyfold, some thirtyfold. (Matthew 13:3–8)

When his disciples were puzzled, he explained that he was referring to God's word being received and understood to varying degrees, and he elaborated (Matthew 13:18–23).

In addition to performing healing cures, such as cleansing lepers (Luke 17:11–19), Jesus demonstrated miraculous powers, including calming a storm (Mark 4:35–39), multiplying five loaves and two fishes to feed five thousand (Luke 9:10–17), walking on water (Matthew 14:25–27), changing water to wine (John 2:1–11), and raising Lazarus from the dead (John 11:38–44), among others.

Jesus' ministry lasted only some three years. Jewish religious leaders began to fear a rebellion, saying of Jesus, "If we let him thus alone, all men will believe in him: and the Romans shall come and take away both our place and nation" (John 11:48). Caiaphas, the high priest, supposedly stated, "it is expedient for us, that one man should die for the people, and that the whole nation perish not" (John 11:50).

The four Gospels all begin their account of Jesus' final week with his triumphal entry into Jerusalem riding on a colt, his path strewn by palm branches—an event now celebrated by Christians as Palm Sunday. The rest occurs in quick succession, with the Gospels differing only in the details: Jesus gathers his twelve disciples for a Last Supper; is betrayed by Judas, who leads armed men to arrest Jesus as he prays in the Garden of Gethsemane; is tried twice (once before the Jewish priesthood and again before Pontius Pilate, the Roman procurator); and is then scourged, crucified, and buried in a tomb.

The central tenet of Christianity—that Jesus was resurrected from the dead—is then related by the four evangelists, with John's Gospel giving the greatest detail. The tomb is discovered empty with the burial linens lying about, and Jesus subsequently makes several appearances to his followers. Then, according to Mark (16:19) and Luke (24:51), Jesus ascends into heaven.

The Nazarene

Those seeking the historical Jesus have little to work from. The Gospels were composed some seventy to a hundred years after Jesus' birth (Ward 1987, 14), creating difficulties from the outset. Mark, whose Gospel was probably the earliest and certainly the shortest, seems to have known nothing of the birth or childhood of Jesus, and neither does John. Luke says that Jesus was born during a census, and the only one historically known occurred in A.D. 6 and 7—a date too late to accord with the other events (baptism, crucifixion) in Jesus' life (Craveri 1967, 33). Matthew asserts that Jesus was born during the reign of King Herod, who died in March of 4 B.C. Thus Jesus' birth occurred some time previous to Herod's death, and scholars generally give the date as between 4 and 11 B.C. (Craveri 1967, 34).

Even Jesus' birthplace is questioned. Matthew is repeatedly at pains to fulfill Old Testament prophecies regarding the Messiah, but one placed the birth at Bethlehem (Micah 5:2), another foretold Egypt (Hosea 11:1), and still another prophesied Nazareth (Judges 13:5). What was Matthew the storyteller to do? He thus has Jesus being born in Bethlehem; then fleeing with his parents to Egypt, so that he can later come "out of Egypt," as the old text decreed; and finally being raised in Nazareth (see figure I.2). Only Matthew (2:7–20) tells the story of the family's flight to Egypt to avoid the slaughter of infants ordered by King Herod (73?–4 B.C.), a historically unknown and unlikely event. The prophecy from Hosea 11:1 ("Out of Egypt have I called my Son") is clearly a reference to Moses and the Exodus, possibly introduced, suggests Asimov (1969, 135), "only so that Matthew could indulge in his favorite exercise of quoting Old Testament verse, for Jesus' stay in Egypt is not referred to in any other place in the New Testament." Mark's knowledge may have represented all that was passed down: "In those days Jesus came from Nazareth of Galilee" (Mark 1:9).

From a historical viewpoint, precious little is known about Jesus. According to biblical scholar Jaroslav Jan Pelikan (*Encyclopaedia Britannica* 1960, s.v. "Jesus Christ"):

> To the modern reader, accustomed to think of the important role that Jesus has played in the history of the world during the past centuries, it may be surprising to realize that few of His contemporaries even took notice of Him. The Jewish historian Josephus seems to refer to Him, although at least one of the passages mentioning Jesus is a later addition, possibly even a Christian forgery. The Roman historian Tacitus and the Roman man of letters Pliny the Younger make mention of Jesus in discussing the treatment of the early Christians. A dubious passage in the Roman historian Suetonius may mean "Jesus Christ" by "Chresto," though it is quite clear that he did not understand it that way. The major purpose served by these non-Christian references to Jesus is to stress how provincial and limited a role He actually played in His own lifetime.

Nevertheless, the case for the historical Jesus is made in Gerd Lüdemann's *Jesus after 2000 Years* (2001, 686):

> Jesus grew up in a circle of more than five brothers and sisters in the Galilean village of Nazareth. He was probably the oldest. His mother tongue was Aramaic, but this does not rule out the possibility that he understood some bits of Greek. He learned a building craft from his father. Like most of his contemporaries, he could not read or write. But the local synagogue near his home was the place of his religious education. Here and on other occasions he learned parts of the Torah by word of mouth: commandments, prophetic instructions and predictions, and exciting stories from the scriptures, for example the narratives about Elijah and Elisha, the prophets who did miracles, which excited many of the pious people of that time.

Lüdemann (2001, 691–92) continues:

Figure I.2. The Holy Family—Mary, Joseph, and the young Jesus—are depicted in an old wood engraving.

Jesus had experienced great success in Galilee. The crowds had responded to his call. Now that same call drew him to Jerusalem. There he wanted to call on the people and its leaders to repent. He marched to Jerusalem, accompanied by a host of disciples, men and women. In a symbolic action he expressed his hope for the new temple in the temple forecourt by overturning some tables of money changers and traders. The Jewish aristocracy could not forgive him that. What happened next bore no similarity to the occasional clashes between Pharisees and Jesus in Galilee. Whereas there Jesus had received no more than insults, here in Jerusalem things were in real earnest. Jesus was slandered as political king of the Jews, and Pilate made short shrift of him. Evidently Jesus had not prepared his disciples well for this. Otherwise they would not all have fled. Finally on the cross, Jesus became the victim in a criminal setting. He suffered here for something which he had neither attempted nor desired. Things had turned out differently from what he had told his disciples and the Jewish people. But probably he had not seen it like that. Here . . . a look at the apostle Paul helps; when Paul observed that Jesus had failed to return, he did not give up his faith because people were dying, but held on to it all the more strongly. He came to the conclusion that whether he lived or died he belonged to the "Lord." That is how Jesus must have thought and felt on the cross, surrendering himself to his Father. No faith can ever be refuted by reality, let alone by arguments.

The Mythologized Jesus

At the end of the nineteenth century, some critics contended quite seriously that Jesus was an entirely legendary figure who had never lived at all. The story the Gospels told, they maintained, was simply a Christian version of a myth about a deity who appeared for a time on earth in human form—like the Egyptian god Osiris, for example (Price 2003, 286–89; *Encyclopaedia Britannica* 1960, s.v. "Jesus Christ"). Certainly, stories of Jesus' magical prowess increased after his death, and in the catacombs he was often portrayed with a magician's wand (Smith 1973, 107).

As noted earlier, the Gospels say little about Jesus' early years. Modern biblical critics tend to be skeptical of all stories about the young Jesus, including such apocryphal accounts as the First Gospel of the Infancy of Jesus Christ, where he is a sort of boy wonder. For example, he brings to life some sparrows he fashioned out of clay, and when a schoolmaster lifts his hand to whip Jesus for refusing to recite his schoolwork, Jesus causes the teacher's hand to wither (1 Infancy 19:19, 20:15, in *Lost Books* 1976).

Rationalists suspect that, as part of the mythologizing process, miracle claims were reported that were based on little or no evidence. Indeed, many seem to have been derived from earlier parallels in the Old Testament. For instance, Jesus' changing of the jars of water to wine (John 2:1–14) follows Moses' transformation of a bowl of water into blood (Exodus 4:9, 30–31). Likewise, Jesus' feeding of the multitudes, related in all four Gospels, is strikingly similar to the feat of Elisha, who fed a hundred men with just a sack of barley loaves and ears of grain (2 Kings 4:43–44). Significantly, the raising of Lazarus from the dead (John 11:38–44) duplicates a resurrection by the prophet Elijah (1 Kings 17:17–24). One writer says of Lazarus' raising that "it is only a preview of Jesus' own miraculous resurrection; therefore the two are one" (Graham 1975, 337). (See figure I.3.)

Similarly, from a modern perspective, critics say that the healing of the sick can be compared with the supposed cures performed by today's faith healers—attributable to the power of suggestion, the body's own healing mechanisms, and other effects—and suitably exaggerated in the narratives (Nickell 1993, 131–66). Interestingly, Jesus' exorcisms—the most frequent miracles in the synoptic Gospels—are completely missing from John (Dummelow 1951, 773).

Further, except for a pious forgery (the purported "Acts of Pilate," produced in the fourth century), there is no record of Jesus' sensational trial in the imperial archives in Rome, although such a record would have been mandatory (Craveri 1967, 407). Although Pontius Pilate was a historical personage—the Roman procurator of Judea (A.D. 26?–36?)—his supposed custom of releasing a prisoner during each Passover feast, as he allegedly did with Barabbas (Matthew 27:15–23), cannot be substantiated. It is highly unlikely that the Romans had such a custom, although it is possible. The detail of

Figure I.3. Jesus is depicted raising Lazarus from the dead—a foreshadowing of his own resurrection (mid-nineteenth-century illustration by Julius Schnorr von Carolsfeld).

Pilate's avowal of innocence in Jesus' death, symbolized by the washing of his hands in public (Matthew 27:24), is an obvious derivation from Deuteronomy (21:6–7).

Regarding the Crucifixion of Jesus, the account in Mark—which, as Price (2003, 321) observes, is the basis for the other Gospel accounts—is clearly derived from Psalm 22, along with a few other texts. Jesus' exclamation—"My God, my God, why hast thou forsaken me?"—comes verbatim from Psalm 22, as do the piercing of the hands and feet, the casting of lots for the garments, and other story motifs.

As for Jesus' resurrection, critics see the motif of the empty tomb as an unlikely—if narratively irresistible—story element. According to Craveri (1967, 425), "In all probability, the Nazarene was buried by the Romans in a common grave with the two thieves." The post-resurrection appearances of Jesus can be understood as apparitions. The first sighting was by a female visionary, Mary Magdalene, who had been possessed by "seven devils" (Mark 16:9)—a madwoman, in other words. According to Asimov (1969, 239), "Even if she had shown marked improvement under Jesus' influence, the shock of the arrest, trial and crucifixion might well have unhinged her once more and made her an easy target for hallucination."

The Physical Evidence

Whatever view one takes of the life of Jesus—religious, historical, mythical, or some combination of these—the fact remains that an astonishing amount of alleged physical evidence of his life has surfaced over the centuries.

Consider, for example, the Shroud of Turin, reputedly the actual burial cloth of Jesus. If genuine, it would not only prove Jesus' historical existence but also reveal his actual physical appearance through the striking image imprinted on it. Moreover, if the image were indeed caused by a miraculous burst of radiant energy (as even some scientists have suggested), it would offer proof of what is otherwise exclusively a matter of faith: that he was indeed resurrected from the dead.

In the pages that follow, I examine in considerable detail a number of alleged relics of the Christ, all with the potential to address questions surrounding this central figure of Christianity. In addition to relics of his family and followers, I investigate those of his nativity and infancy, life and ministry, and Crucifixion and resurrection, ranging from the purported relics of the wise men to the legendary Holy Grail and artifacts attributed to his death and burial: the True Cross, the holy garments, the lance of Longinus, and various other burial wrappings, supposedly bearing traces of his blood. I also discuss a controversial ossuary not of Jesus but purportedly of his brother, yet bearing Jesus' name written in stone.

I employ a scholarly and scientific method that begins not with preconceived conclusions but with the evidence itself. Thus I hope to avoid the extremes of a too credulous, even mystery-mongering approach, on the one hand, and a dismissive debunking, on the other. The true investigator does not seek to justify his or her prejudices but instead to solve a mystery and so discover the truth. It is not faith but forensic microscopy and serology, for example, that can tell us what substances create the image on the Shroud of Turin.

A skeptical approach helps avoid bias, and objectivity is served by the maxim that extraordinary claims require extraordinary proof. It should also be remembered that the burden of proof—in science, as in a court of law—is on the one who asserts some fact or advocates an idea; it is not up to someone else to disprove the claim. In the case of competing hypotheses, we can apply the principle of Occam's razor (after William of Ockham, a fourteenth-century philosopher), which affirms that the simplest explanation—that is, the hypothesis that relies on the fewest assumptions—is most likely correct. This approach can spare us from error and from the unfortunate circumstance of the blindfolded leading the blind. So, in the spirit of free inquiry, I investigate and seek to shed light on the mystery that is Jesus.

CHAPTER 1

The Cult of Relics

A relic is an object that was once connected with the body of a saint, martyr, or other holy person (see figure 1.1). In Christianity, veneration of relics appeared early in both Eastern and Western church practices (*Encyclopaedia Britannica* 1960, s.v. "Relics").

The Origin of Relics

Early Christians believed that the bodies of the dead—or, by extension, objects that had touched them—had special qualities or powers that made them worthy of veneration. This was based on the concept of beneficent contagion:

> Its basis is the idea that man's virtue, or holiness, or protective healing powers, do not die with him; they continue to reside in his body and can be tapped by any believer who in some way makes contact with his corporeal shrine. Mere proximity is enough: the medieval pilgrim was satisfied if he could but gaze on the tomb of his cult-object. . . .
>
> If the body is dismembered, so the belief goes on, the power within it is not diminished; on the contrary, each part will be as full of potency as the whole. The same thing applies to anything that the cult object touched while alive or, indeed, to anything that touches him after he is dead. All these inanimate containers of a supposedly animate force—whole bodies, bones, hair and teeth, clothes, books, furniture, instruments of martyrdom, winding-sheets, coffins and (if the body is cremated) the ashes that are left—are dignified by the

Figure 1.1. A portion of the vast collection of relics of saints kept in the Church of Maria Ausiliatrice in Turin, Italy (photo by Stefano Bagnasco).

name of "relics" and credited with the grace that once resided in their owners. (Pick 1979, 101)

The impulse to keep a relic may simply begin as an act of respect for a beloved person. For example, when Buddha died and was cremated, in about 483 B.C., his bones were reputedly saved by some Indian monks. Subsequently, a few pieces were taken to China, where a finger bone was discovered beneath a temple in 1987. In 2004, in what some saw as a "propaganda exercise," China loaned the relic—displayed in a bulletproof glass container—to Hong Kong Buddhists for Buddha's birthday celebration (Wong 2004). Primarily, however, the veneration of Buddha's relics is intended to engender faith and acquire spiritual merit, although legends of miracles have sprung up (*Encyclopaedia Britannica* 1978, s.v. "Relics, Buddhist").

The Old Testament makes specific reference to the veneration of relics. The religious character of a saintly person's remains is acknowledged, for instance, in the burial of Rachel, the wife of Jacob: "And Rachel died, and was buried in the way of Ephrath, which is Bethlehem. And Jacob set a pillar upon her grave: that is the pillar of Rachel's grave unto this day" (Genesis 35:19–20). There is also a reference to Joseph's relics: "And Joseph took an oath of the children of Israel, saying God will surely visit you, and ye shall carry up my bones from hence. So Joseph died, being an hundred and ten years old: and they embalmed him, and he was put in a coffin in Egypt" (Genesis 50:25–26).

The Old Testament also refers to the miraculous power of a relic that was employed by Elisha:

> He took up also the mantle of Elijah that fell from him, and went back, and stood by the bank of Jordan; and he took the mantle of Elijah that fell from him, and smote the waters, and said, "Where is the Lord God of Elijah?" And when he had also smitten the waters, they parted hither and thither: and Elisha went over.
>
> And when the sons of the prophets which were to view at Jericho saw him, they said, "The spirit of Elijah doth rest on Elisha." And they came to meet him, and bowed themselves to the ground before him. (2 Kings 2:13–15)

Like the mantle of Elijah, the relics of Elisha would come to work miracles, according to a later passage: "And it came to pass, as they were burying a man, that, behold, they spied a band of men; and they cast the man into the sepulchre of Elisha: and when the man was let down, and touched the bones of Elisha, he revived, and stood up on his feet" (2 Kings 13:21). This portrayal of Elisha as a potent magician—who could use the inherited mantle of Elijah to part Jordan's waters and whose own bones could miraculously revive a dead man—sets the stage for the later miraculous relics of Jesus. This is not surprising, because in many ways, Jesus was seen as a successor to Elisha. For example, the story of Jesus' miraculous multiplication of the loaves (Mark 6:34–44) follows a similar feat attributed to Elisha (2 Kings 4:42–44) (Metzger and Coogan 2001, 139).

The Veneration of Relics

Despite these Old Testament examples, there is little justification in either the Old or the New Testament to support what would become a cult of relics in early Christianity. Indeed, according to the *New Catholic Encyclopedia* (1967, s.v. "Relics"): "In the Apocalypse [or Revelation] the author recommends that the faithful and martyrs be left to rest in peace (11:13). Despite this, although the Apostles inherited Jewish diffidence regarding relics, the new converts in the time of St. Paul disputed about objects that belonged to the Apostles and recognized as miraculous agents clothing that they had touched (Acts 19:12)." This refers to Paul's healing powers: "And God wrought special miracles by the hands of Paul: So that from his body were brought unto the sick handkerchiefs or aprons, and the diseases departed from them, and the evil spirits went out of them" (Acts 19:11–12).

The earliest veneration of Christian relics can be traced to around A.D. 156, when Polycarp, the bishop of Smyrna (later St. Polycarp), was martyred. He was to be burned at the stake, but the fire blazed poorly, so he was stabbed to death instead. His body was then burned, after which his followers sought to take his remains. Although they encountered some resistance, they eventually "took up his bones,

Figure 1.2. The focal point of the relic chapel in the Church of Maria Ausiliatrice in Turin is a lighted cross with a purported piece of the True Cross (photo by author).

which are more valuable than precious stones and finer than refined gold, and laid them in a suitable place, where the Lord will permit us to gather ourselves together, as we are able, in gladness and joy, and to celebrate the birthday of his martyrdom" (*Catholic Encyclopedia* 1911, s.v. "Relics"; Coulson 1958, 383).

Sometime after the death of St. Polycarp (exactly when is not known), the distribution and veneration of tiny fragments of bone, cloth, packets of dust, and the like became common. The practice was widespread in the early fourth century. Sometime before 350, pieces of wood allegedly from the True Cross, discovered circa 318, had been distributed throughout the Christian world (*Catholic Encyclopedia* 1911, s.v. "Relics"). (See figure 1.2.)

The early church fathers happily tolerated relic worship. As paganism retreated, according to historian Edward Gibbon (1737–1794):

It must be ingenuously confessed that the ministers of the Catholic Church imitated the profane models which they were impatient to destroy. The most respectable bishops had persuaded themselves that the ignorant rustics would more cheerfully renounce the superstitions of paganism, if they found some resemblance, some compensation in the bosom of Christianity. The religion of Constantine achieved, in less than a century, the final conquest of the Roman Empire: but the victors themselves were insensibly subdued by the arts of their vanquished rivals. (quoted in Meyer 1971, 73)

No less a figure than St. Thomas Aquinas (1225–1274) set forth the doctrinal principles on which relic veneration is based:

It is clear . . . that he who has a certain affection for anyone, venerates whatever of his is left after death, not only his body and the parts thereof, but even external things, such as his clothes and such-like. Now it is manifest that we should show honour to the saints of God, as being members of Christ, and children and friends of God, and our intercessors. Wherefore in memory of them we ought to honour any relics of theirs in a fitting manner: principally their bodies, which were temples, and organs of the Holy Spirit dwelling and operating in them, and are destined to be likened to the body of Christ by the glory of the resurrection. Hence God Himself fittingly honours such relics by working miracles at their presence. (Aquinas 1273)

From a modern scientific point of view, such an attribute is rooted in superstition—an explanation of both its appeal (to the emotional rather than the rational) and its potential for abuse.

The Dispensation of Relics

In the fourth and fifth centuries, the veneration of the relics of martyrs expanded in the form of a liturgical cult, receiving theological justification. Martyrs' tombs were opened, and relics were subsequently distributed as *brandea*—objects that had been touched to the body or bones. These were placed in little cases that were worn around the neck (*New Catholic Encyclopedia* 1967, s.v. "Relics").

Christian saints' relics are divided into four classes:

1. A first-class relic is either the body of a saint or a portion of it, such as a piece of bone or fragment of flesh.

2. A second-class relic is an item or piece of an item that was used by a saint, such as an article of clothing.
3. A third-class relic is an item that was deliberately touched to a first-class relic.
4. A fourth-class relic is anything that was deliberately touched to a second-class relic with the intent of creating a fourth-class relic.

First- and second-class relics were especially revered, whereas third- and fourth-class relics could be given away or sold to individuals.

Relics provided a concise link between tombs and altars. As the saints' tombs became pilgrimage sites, churches were erected there to enshrine the relics and promote devotion to the local saints. An example is the Vatican's Basilica of St. Peter, which was built over the apostle's reputed grave (Woodward 1990, 57).

In the year 410, the Council of Carthage ordered local bishops to destroy any altar that had been set up as a memorial to a martyr and to prohibit the building of any new shrine unless it contained a relic or was built on a site made holy by the person's life or death (Woodward 1990, 59). By 767, the cult of saints had become entrenched, and the Council of Nicaea declared that all church altars must contain an altar stone that held a saint's relics. To this day, the Catholic Church's Code of Canon Law defines an altar as a "tomb containing the relics of a saint" (Woodward 1990, 59). The practice of placing a relic in each church altar continued until 1969 (Christian relics 2004).

Acquisition of an important relic could justify the building of an elegant repository in which to house it. For instance, when the residents of Amiens acquired a piece of John the Baptist's head in 1206, they resolved to erect France's largest church. By 1220, they had gathered the necessary resources, and "the noble vault of the cathedral was steadily rising" (Tuchman 1978, 12).

The practice of placing relics on exhibition was authorized during the ninth century, but not until the thirteenth century were reliquaries—containers used to keep or display relics— placed permanently on (or more often behind) the altar (*Catholic Encyclopedia* 1907, s.v.

"Altar"). Reliquaries appear in an impressive variety of forms, including boxes, caskets, shrines, and the like, and they are typically ornate, often made of silver or gold and commonly bejeweled (see figure 1.3). For example, a French casket of the twelfth or thirteenth century depicts a crucified Christ and other holy personages in Limoges enamel on copper, studded with gems. Another reliquary contains the Holy Thorn set in a gemstone and surrounded by an enameled scene of the Last Judgment, with many figures in full relief and bearing the arms of John, duke of Berry (circa 1389–1407). A Venetian glass reliquary, stemmed like a goblet and surmounted with a glass cover, dates from the late sixteenth century. (See *Encyclopaedia Britannica* 1960, s.v. "Romanesque Art," "Enamel," "Glass.") In the fourteenth century, King Charles V of France collected incredible relics that he kept in gem-studded reliquaries in his royal chapel. These included a fragment of Moses' rod, a flask containing the Virgin's milk, Jesus' swaddling clothes, and other alleged relics, including many related to the Crucifixion (Tuchman 1978, 237).

One type of reliquary, known as a monstrance, typically consisted of a metal-framed, cylindrical crystal case mounted on a stand. It was originally used to expose sacred relics to view, but over time, it became the vessel in which the Host, or consecrated wafer, is carried in processions for veneration by the faithful (*Encyclopaedia Britannica* 1960, s.v. "Monstrance"). Another distinct type of reliquary took the shape of a forearm and a hand, mounted upright on a base. These hand reliquaries had small glass windows, typically located on the ornately fashioned "sleeve," that held bits of bone or other relics. Some featured two fingers upraised in the familiar gesture of benediction; these usually represented a bishop or abbot-saint, "since they retained their earthly status along with their healing powers after death" (Piece of the week 2001). Other reliquaries took the form of a leg or a bust. In Naples Cathedral, for example, is a silver bust of St. Januarius that reputedly holds the legendary martyr's skull (Rogo 1982, 192).

Relic veneration continues within Catholic and Orthodox Christianity, but it was rejected by the Protestant Reformation and by

Figure 1.3. Ornate reliquary of the reputed blood of Christ is displayed in a basilica in Bruges, Belgium (from an old postcard).

most of today's Protestants (Christian relics 2004). With the closure of Latin monasteries and convents in 1962, and as relic holders, such as priests, have died, relics have found their way onto the open market. An organization has been formed to reclaim them. Called Christian Relic Rescue (CRR), it was founded in 2002 and "obtains (usually through purchase) as many First and Second Class Relics of Christian Saints as possible from auctioneers, antique dealers, and unauthorized individuals for the purpose of placing the Relics *at no cost*, in Faith Communities where they receive the Christian veneration for which they were intended" (Relics in Christian faith 2005).

Authentication

The sale of relics had become so prevalent in the time of St. Augustine (about 400) that he deplored "hypocrites in the garb of monks for hawking about of the limbs of martyrs," adding skeptically, "if indeed [they are] of martyrs" (*Encyclopaedia Britannica* 1978, s.v. "Relics") (see figure 1.4). At about the same time, Vigilantius of Toulouse

Figure 1.4. Reputed relic of St. Augustine—ironically, a skeptic of many relics—is kept in a locket-type reliquary (author's collection).

condemned the veneration of relics, which he regarded as pure idolatry. St. Jerome, however, attempted to defend the cult—in part, on the grounds that God worked miracles through saints' relics (*New Catholic Encyclopedia* 1967, s.v. "Relics"). According to one writer (Meyer 1971, 73):

> So widespread and insistent was the demand for relics that in the ninth century a specialized corporation was formed in Rome to discover, sell and transport holy relics to all parts of Europe. . . . Roman catacombs were ransacked for old bones, which were duly identified with suitable saints. Some became hydra-headed—a number of churches claimed to have the skull of John the Baptist.

An old joke tells of a pilgrim's response to seeing a second head of John the Baptist. When he asked how this could be, he was told, "The other one was from when he was a boy."

Relics of the Old Testament prophets were discovered retrospectively as well. In addition to Moses' rod were pieces of the stone tablets on which God supposedly wrote the Ten Commandments (see figure 1.5). There were also the slippers of the patriarch Enoch,

Figure 1.5. Fragments of the tablets of the Ten Commandments were among the alleged relics of Old Testament prophets. Here the tablets are shown being given to Moses by God (mid-nineteenth-century illustration by Julius Schnorr von Carolsfeld).

as well as the hem of Joseph's coat of many colors. An English cathedral had a sprig of the burning bush from which God had instructed Moses. There were also various relics of the prophet Daniel, and so on—a continuous commentary on human credulity (Nickell 1998, 50–51; Gies and Gies 1990, 295).

Bogus relics were often accompanied by supposed evidence of their authenticity. For example, St. Briocus of Great Britain yielded several relics—two ribs, an arm, and a vertebra—along with "proof" that they were genuinely miraculous: when they were placed in a church at Angers, they supposedly "jumped for joy at the honor conferred upon them" (Brewer 1884, 261–62). Similarly, the hand of St.

William of Oulx, a one-armed peasant, reportedly refused burial by repeatedly pushing itself through the coffin; it was finally severed and retained as a relic known as the Angelic Hand (Nickell 1998, 50–51).

Relic fakery had become so rampant in the fourteenth century that Geoffrey Chaucer (1340?–1400) satirized the practice in his *Canterbury Tales,* a narrative of the stories told by pilgrims as they wend their way from the Tabard Inn in Southwark to Canterbury Cathedral. One of the stories, "The Pardoner's Tale," is that of a hypocritical ecclesiastic whose profession is to raise money by selling pardons or indulgences (remissions of temporal punishment due for sins). Chaucer's pardoner also engages in relic magic, claiming that he has a sheep's bone that once belonged to a "holy Jew" and, when washed in any well, produces water with curative power for man or beast. When the pardoner offers to let the inn's host kiss certain holy relics he keeps in his wallet, the host retorts, "Thow woldest make me kiss thyn olde breech [i.e., breechcloth or drawers] And swere it were a relyk of a seint" (Dunn 1952, 171).

In his classic book of travel sketches, *The Innocents Abroad,* Mark Twain delights in satirizing some of the outrageous purported relics he encounters. About the Tomb of Adam in the Holy Land, Twain comments in wry fashion, "There is no question that he is actually buried in the grave which is pointed out as his—there can be none—because it has never yet been proven that that grave is not the grave in which he is buried" (Twain 1869, 402–3, 423). Twain catalogs a great number of Christian relics, commenting, "Relics are very good property. Travelers are expected to pay for seeing them, and they do it cheerfully. We like the idea. One's conscience can never be the worse for the knowledge that he has paid his way like a man" (393–94).

The Catholic Church has not addressed the question of authenticity in a head-on fashion. It often sidesteps the issue by not taking a position on the genuineness of a particular relic. The veneration of certain doubtful relics has been permitted to continue on the grounds that, even if a relic is in fact spurious, God is not dishonored by an error made in good faith; besides, it is difficult to reach a final verdict in the case of many relics. And, it is argued, devotions "deeply rooted in the heart of peasantry" cannot be dismissed lightly (Christian relics 2004). Thus an end-justifies-the-means attitude—which helped create and promote fake relics in the first place—has prevailed.

Many of the faithful have even given credence to certain "holy persons" who claimed to be able to discern whether a relic was genuine or false. One was Anne Catherine Emmerich (1774–1824), on whose "visions" the movie *The Passion of the Christ* was largely based (Nickell 2004c). Emmerich also claimed to be able to identify a relic's nature and origin. Another was the suspect stigmatic Therese Neumann (1898–1962), who also allegedly wept bloody tears, experienced visions of the Virgin Mary, and avoided all food and drink except for daily Communion, in addition to other showy feats (Nickell 1993, 223, 228). During certain "ecstasies," Neumann could allegedly divine the truth about relics (Cruz 1984, 8). Needless to say, none of these holy clairvoyants was ever tested scientifically.

CHAPTER 2

Christian Relics

Supposed physical traces of Jesus were paramount to the cult of relics, but so were those of his family and followers. This chapter examines relics related to Jesus' nativity and infancy, his subsequent life and ministry, his disciples, and the saints that came later.

Nativity and Infancy

Relics supposedly related to the birth and early years of Jesus were conveniently discovered retroactively. Germany claimed to have relics of the three wise men, including their gifts to the Christ child (Nickell 1998, 51). "Wise men from the east" are referred to only in Matthew (2:1), but there is no mention of how many there were. In Eastern tradition there were twelve, but because only three gifts were presented—gold, frankincense, and myrrh—Western tradition limited the wise men to that number; later, their names were given as Balthasar, Melchior, and Caspar. They are sometimes referred to as three kings, but the Greek word for *magi* refers to eastern magicians; that they might be astrologers is suggested by their following a star to Bethlehem (Metzger and Coogan 2001, 188).

A cathedral in Cologne boasted the Magi's skulls, or, as one devotee described them, "the crowned heads of the three holy kings." They are still there, kept in a reliquary decorated with jewels and cameos. According to legend, the relics were discovered by St. Helena, mother of Constantine the Great (280?–337), and were later transferred to Milan, Italy, by St. Eustorgio (d. 518) in an oxcart. After Milan fell to Frederick Barbarossa in 1162, they were transported to Cologne in 1164 (Cruz 1984, 154; Lowenthal 1998). It appears, however, that the entire Milan episode was fabricated by Rainald, archbishop of Cologne (Lowenthal 1998).

In 1909, some fragments of the reputed Magi bones were "returned" to Milan, where they are enshrined in the church named for their legendary transporter, the sixth-century bishop of Milan. I visited the Basilica of St. Eustorgio (see figures 2.1 and 2.2) in 2004 with journalist and investigative writer Massimo Polidoro, a great friend and guide. In a dark recess of the church we read the inscription "SEPVLCRVM TRIVM MAGORVM" (Sepulchre of the Three Magi). A carved stone slab nearby is accompanied by a sign that states, "According to tradition this stone slab with the comet was on top of the Magi's tomb and was brought to Italy along with their relics." While we were there, the faithful offered devotions to the various relics of Christ, including the Holy Lance, the veronica, and others (discussed in later chapters).

At Rome's Basilica of St. Mary Major is an elaborate reliquary containing five age-blackened boards, four of which are reputed to be from the holy manger or crib. The fifth bears an artist's notes, in Greek, regarding some religious figures yet to be sculpted. The devoutly credulous author of *Relics*, Joan Carroll Cruz (1984, 22), writes:

> The crib or manger in which the Child Jesus was placed after His birth is thought to have been the place in the stable where food for domestic animals was placed, and is believed to have been hewn from the limestone of the cave walls. One theory is that the four boards were used as supports for the limestone manger, two on each end in the form of an X. Another theory is that the shape of the wood suggests that when fitted together with certain additional parts, they would have formed a proper bottom for a crib.

Interestingly, all five boards are fastened together by two strips of metal, which, to Cruz, "suggest an ancient assembly." If so, given

(Left) Figure 2.1. Basilica of St. Eustorgio in Milan purportedly contains relics and a tomb slab of the Magi (photo by author).

(Below) Figure 2.2. Depiction of the Magi giving gifts to the Christ child over the door of the Basilica of St. Eustorgio in Milan (photo by author).

the fifth annotated board, one might suspect that an old artist's box, rack, or other item had been foisted off on gullible clerics and, in turn, unsuspecting pilgrims.

Although there is no mention of the preservation of Jesus' relics in the New Testament, there are references to them in certain apocryphal Gospels. The First Gospel of the Infancy of Jesus Christ claims that an "old Hebrew woman" kept the infant Jesus' foreskin (or perhaps the umbilical cord; the story's author is unsure). This was allegedly preserved "in an alabaster box of old oil of spikenard," said to be the very ointment later used to anoint Jesus' head and feet prior to the events leading up to the Crucifixion (1 Infancy 2:2, in *Lost Books* 1976). Jesus' foreskin was ubiquitous. Voltaire took delight in noting that no fewer than six churches had it (Meyer 1971, 73). At least one survives, kept in a jewel-studded reliquary held aloft by sculpted angels (Nickell 1998, 51).

Other messages from the Gospel of the Infancy claim that the baby's swaddling clothes worked magic. On one occasion, the clothes were instrumental in exorcising a youth's devils, which flew from his mouth "in the shape of crows and serpents." In another instance, they burst into flames and frightened away a "dreadful dragon" (which was Satan in disguise); it was found that one of the cloths was impervious to fire.

At least one of Jesus' swaddling garments purportedly survives, kept in a golden reliquary at Aix-la-Chapelle, the shrine built by Charlemagne (742–814) in Aachen, Germany. (The reliquary was originally intended for the arm of St. Simeon.) Reportedly, the relic was one of several brought from the Holy Land and Rome and secured by Charlemagne when he built the cathedral (Cruz 1984, 23).

In Constantinople (present-day Istanbul, Turkey) the mosque of St. Sophia boasted additional treasures of the baby Jesus. "Amongst others," reported freethinker D. M. Bennett (1882, 669), "an excavated block of red marble is shown as the cradle of Jesus in his infancy, and nearby it is a basin in which Jesus is said to have been washed by his mother." Bennett adds, "Both are claimed to have been brought from Bethlehem, but nobody believes it save overcredulous Mohammedans."

Other relics of the nativity include hay from the manger and some of the babe's hair, as well as his pap spoon and dish, his umbilical cord, his milk teeth, and the cloak with which Joseph covered the infant at Bethlehem (Nickell 1998, 51). About one of the alleged baby teeth, the French Benedictine monk and historian Guibert of Nogent (1053–1124) wondered skeptically, "How did anyone think to save it?" (On hearing about a second head of John the Baptist, Guibert asked sarcastically, "Was this saint then bicephalous?" [Gies and Gies, 1990, 294–95].)

Among other remarkable relics were those of Joseph and Mary, including Joseph's girdle, staff, and hammer. Various plows fashioned in his carpentry shop and worked on by the young Jesus were described by Justin Martyr (100?–165), who claimed to have heard of them in Palestine. Craveri (1967, 60) calls this story "barely credible."

Some of Mary's hair was preserved, together with vials of her breast milk. Also gathered were chips of rock on which a few drops of her milk had legendarily fallen, turning the rock white and imbuing it with curative powers. At Loretto, in Italy, pilgrims visited the house where Mary had lived at the time of the Annunciation (Luke 1:26–35); it had miraculously been transported from Nazareth to this Italian site (Nickell 1998, 51–52). "Some very astonishing relics" of the Annunciation also were contained in a monastery at Mount Athos in Greece. These consisted of "identical feathers which came from the angel Gabriel's wings at the time he visited the Virgin and told her about her being overshadowed by Yahweh, or the Holy Ghost" (Bennett 1882, 616–17). Among other relics of Mary is a length of green ribbon that she supposedly wore as a belt, but it has no historical record prior to 1141. Known as the Cincture of the Blessed Mother, it is kept in a gold and crystal reliquary in the Cathedral of Prato, Italy (Cruz 1984, 60).

Another edifice, the Cathedral of Chartres, France, owns a garment known variously as the *Sainte Chemisa* (Holy Shirt), *S. Tunica B.V.M.* (Holy Tunic of the Blessed Virgin Mary), and *Voile de la Vierge* (Veil of the Virgin). Although it is often represented as a sort of chemise, it is actually only a seamless length of cloth. Its provenance is unknown before 876. Other European churches also have pieces of cloth that reputedly come from a veil belonging to the Virgin. These may derive from the Chartres cloth, which was divided on September 24, 1793, during the French Revolution. The largest piece was retained by the church, and smaller pieces were distributed to those present (Cruz 1984, 63–65).

One church—the Cathedral of Aachen, Germany—even has the Marian counterpart of the Shroud of Turin: the Shroud of Our Lady, the reputed burial cloth of the Virgin. Kept in a golden shrine, the cloth is exhibited only at seven-year intervals, when pilgrims flock to the city for the purpose of viewing the alleged relic and its expensive reliquary (Cruz 1984, 65).

Some relics of Mary seem especially tenuous. One is a chair covered in blue velvet and kept in the Chapel of the Motherhouse in Paris. Supposedly, during an apparitional visit to visionary Catherine Labouré in 1830, the Virgin sat in the chair. Visitors to the chapel are permitted to touch the chair and to leave on its seat small papers on which they have written their requests for divine favors (Cruz 1984, 61–62).

Life and Ministry

The purported relics commemorating the events of Jesus' ministry include a tear that he supposedly shed at the tomb of Lazarus, the brother of Martha and Mary. According to the Gospel of John, Lazarus had been buried four days when Jesus arrived. He was so moved by the grief of Lazarus' sisters and others that, according to the shortest verse in the Bible, "Jesus wept" (John 11:35). Hence the relic of the preserved tear, which someone had the foresight, and a convenient vial, to capture. (Jesus then raised Lazarus, who emerged from his tomb—a cave with a stone over it—in his burial clothes, foreshadowing Jesus' own resurrection.)

Relics of Lazarus were reputedly kept in the Cathedral of St. Lazarus at Autun, France. According to church sources (summarized by Cruz 1984, 155):

The Greek Church believed that sometime after the dispersion of the apostles on their missionary endeavors, and during the early days of the Christian suppression, Lazarus, together with other Christians, was cast adrift by hostile Jews in the hope that they would perish at sea. For this reason the boat was described as being flimsy and leaky. The boat sailed from Jaffa to Larnaca on the island of Cyprus where Lazarus disembarked and lived for more than thirty years. He was eventually buried there after suffering for the Faith. His tomb was miraculously discovered in 899 and his relics brought to Constantinople by order of Emperor Leo VI. The journey of these relics is complicated; however, it has been proved that the cult of Lazarus was in full progress in Autun, France, as early as the 10th century. The relics were first venerated in the Church of St. Nazaire where they rested in a sarcophagus to the right of the high altar. A short distance from this church another church was built and dedicated to St. Lazarus. Consecrated by Pope Innocent II on December 28, 1130, it was later designated a cathedral in 1195.

In time, the relics of Lazarus were transferred to the present shrine bearing his name and placed in a tomb located before the central apse. Cruz (1984, 155) reports, "In the 18th century the tomb was dismantled and the pieces sold for reasons not specified. Whether or not the relics are retained by the cathedral is unclear."

In addition to the tear shed at Lazarus' tomb, the Christian faithful have been able to view, at one time or another, other relics of Jesus' life and ministry: one of the vessels in which he miraculously changed water to wine at a marriage feast at Cana (John 2:1–11), the tail of the ass he rode into Jerusalem (John 12:12–15), and a lock of hair from the woman who lovingly washed his feet with her tears and dried them with her tresses (Luke 7:44) (Nickell 1998, 52). At Troyes, in north-central France, the cathedral treasury displays what is reputed to be the very basin in which Jesus washed the feet of his disciples (John 13:5–15).

Among other relics associated with Jesus is "one of the Biblical sower's wheat seeds" (Gies and Gies 1990, 294–95)—which is curious, because the sower was only a character in a parable that Jesus told to his disciples (Matthew 13:3–30, Mark 4:3–20, Luke 8:4–15). Jesus' "seamless coat" is claimed by two churches. Although both are historically suspect, some argue that one could be the garment touchéd by the woman who desired healing, as related in Mark (5:28–30), and the other could be the one the Roman soldiers cast lots for at the Crucifixion (John 19:23–24). (These are discussed in chapter 6.)

Most of the significant relics of Jesus are those relating to the Passion —beginning with the Last Supper and continuing with the Crucifixion, death, and burial. Those relics are presented in later chapters.

Disciples

Relics relating to Jesus' disciples, especially the twelve apostles, were prolific—especially those of St. Peter. The Vatican claimed to have the bones of Peter and Paul early in the third century, and in 258 they were removed to the catacombs (Cruz 1984, 125; *Encyclopaedia Britannica* 1960, s.v. "Peter"). Other relics of Peter include a chair inlaid with ivory, which "may have been added in the ninth century" (Cruz 1984, 126); given its undocumented history, the chair may date from that time as well. The chair and a wooden table used for celebrating Mass allegedly came from a house where Peter lodged when he first came to Rome. His wooden altar is exhibited in the Lateran, the Cathedral Church of Rome, enclosed inside a larger marble altar. The Lateran also holds the reputed heads of Peter and Paul (Cruz 1984, 127–28). Yet Peter's skeleton was allegedly dicsovered and returned to his original tomb, the ceremony being conducted by Pope Paul on June 27, 1968 (Walsh 1985).

Rome also claims to have the chains of St. Peter from one or more of his imprisonments. They are in the Basilica of San Pietro in Vincoli (St. Peter in Chains) beneath the church's high altar, not far from Michelangelo's famous statue *Moses.* The chains are shown in an ornate, golden, glass-paneled urn. Among other relics of Peter are his sandals (kept in the Holy Chamber of the Cathedral of Oviedo, Spain), which cannot be traced back further than about the ninth century (Cruz 1984, 128–29). Still others include parings from his toenails (which reportedly existed in remarkable quantity), "filings" from his chains, and vials of his tears (Nickell 1998, 51; Cruz 1984, 3).

Peter's brother, Andrew, is the subject of a curious phenomenon. His reputed bones are enshrined in Amalfi, Italy, where they produce a "mysterious oil" called *manna*. Reportedly having occurred in three countries—Greece, Turkey, and Italy—where the bones were kept at various times, the manna has appeared in both liquid and powder form (usually the former) allegedly for more than fourteen centuries. The relics are kept within the altar in an urn, beneath which is a silver basin to collect the exudations. It is said that they appear without fail on January 28 (the anniversary of their rediscovery in 1846) and sometimes on other special holidays (Cruz 1984, 192–94). Whether the phenomenon is miraculous, natural, or fraudulent has not been determined by independent scientific investigation.

The bones of St. Andrew at Amalfi do not include his skull. That is enshrined in a silver bust in the church at Patras, Greece, where the apostle is said to have been crucified in A.D. 60 by being bound, rather than nailed, to an X-shaped cross (although, according to Coulson [1958, 29], that form of the cross "does not, in fact, seem to have been associated with the saint before the fourteenth century"). Transferred to St. Peter's in Rome for safekeeping in 1464, the skull was returned to Patras half a millennium later, in 1964, when Pope Paul VI so ordered (Cruz 1984, 106–7).

Legend also connects St. Andrew's relics with Scotland. In the fourth century, the person who guarded Andrew's bones at Patras (St. Rule) had a dream in which he was instructed to take a portion of them to a place that would be revealed to him. That site was what is now St. Andrews on the east coast of Scotland, where he built a church and made converts (Coulson 1958, 29). *The Wordsworth Dictionary of Saints* terms the Scottish claim "dubious," stating that it is more likely that the relics of Andrew were "taken to Constantinople, stolen at its overthrow in the Crusades in 1204 and removed to Amalfi, Italy" (Jones 1994, 22).

The relics of James, son of Zebedee (called St. James the Greater, to distinguish him from the other apostle of that name), became the subject of a pious legend that is indeed remarkable. In the early history of the church, James was among the first disciples to be martyred (Acts 12:1–2); he was executed by King Herod Agrippa I in the year 44. According to one legend, his accuser repented as the execution was about to occur and was beheaded along with James. By the seventh century, another pious tale claimed that James had taken the Gospel to Spain. Subsequently, still another legend told that because Herod had forbidden James' beheaded body to be buried, on the night after the execution, several Christians secretly carried his remains to a ship. Angels then conducted the vessel miraculously to Spain, and the body was transported to the site of the present-day cathedral. The apostle's body lay undiscovered until the early ninth century; then, according to yet another miracle tale, a star led a pious friar to the burial place, whereupon a small basilica was built over the site. The present cathedral there was largely completed in 1128.

The alleged discovery of the relics came at an opportune time. After the Moors conquered Spain, only its northwest corner remained independent, and it was from there that the drive to reconquer the country for Christendom was launched. The supposedly divine revelation of the relics seemed to endorse the quest, and St. James—Santiago—"became the rallying figure for Christian opposition to the Moors" (Jones 1994, 144). Miracles began to occur at the site, more legends were created, and the Cathedral of Santiago de Compostela became one of the most popular of all pilgrimage sites (Nickell 2004a, 100–114).

The relics of St. James, kept in a reliquary in the crypt beneath the church, are the central focus of the shrine and its very raison d'être—but are they genuine? I visited Compostela in 1997 and began an investigation (Nickell 2004a, 100–114). Briefly, I found that the legend of the guiding star had been prompted by a mistranslation. Whereas *Compostella* was thought to derive from *Campus stellae* ("the field of the star"), it more likely came from *Campus stelae* (a *stele* being an inscribed stone), that is, a "field of monuments" or "gravestone field." Another possibility is that *compostela* is simply a diminutive form of *compostum*, "cemetery." Thus, it seems likely that the name originally meant "graveyard" and was mistranslated as "star field"; that mistranslation, in turn, prompted the tale purporting to explain the name. It also seems unlikely that the apostle's remains would have been arduously transported to northern Spain and continue unknown until they were allegedly revealed nearly eight centuries later. *The Penguin Dictionary of Saints* concludes that there is "no evidence whatever as to the identity of the relics" supposedly discovered in ninth-century Spain (Attwater 1983, 179).

There is even a question about the exact nature of the relics. It appears probable that James' body was buried in Jerusalem. Contravening stories surround alleged portions that are housed elsewhere. For example, a shrine at Constantinople held a silver arm containing a relic of James, which was taken to Troyes, France, after the capture of Constantinople in 1204. The saint's hand is supposedly preserved in the abbey in Reading, England, and still another relic is claimed by an Italian cathedral (Nickell 2004a, 107–10).

James the Greater's brother, John the Evangelist, is popularly believed to have written the fourth Gospel (Metzger and Coogan 2001, 153; Jones 1994, 153). According to tradition, he died at an advanced age at Ephesus, Turkey. A little chapel there claims to be the home he shared with the mother of Jesus. It is said that the apostle was buried in what became a side chapel of St. John's Basilica in Ephesus, which is presently in ruins. However, the alleged tomb is indicated by an iron railing and two columns (Cruz 1984, 113–14). Perhaps the most bizarre relic attributed to John was a gold ring he supposedly sent from heaven to St. Colette (or Nicoletta) as proof that Christ had selected her as his virgin bride. She also received from John a crucifix with a small locket containing a piece of the True Cross (Nickell 1998, 51).

Among other relics of the apostles was the reputed finger of doubting Thomas (Nickell 1998, 50). After hearing of the appearance of the risen Christ, he said, "Except I shall see in his hands the print of the nails, and put my finger into the print of the nails, and thrust my hand into his side, I will not believe." But after eight days, Thomas was reportedly present at another apparition, whereupon he touched the wounds and declared, "My Lord and My God" (John 20:24–29). Other relics included the alleged bones of Bartholomew, Philip, James the Less, Matthew, and Simon (Cruz 1984, 107–33); the skull of Philip, contained in a reliquary bearing a bejeweled, golden crown; and Judas' infamous pieces of silver, one of which was in the cathedral treasury of Sens, France (Gies and Gies 1990, 294–95).

Although not one of the apostles, St. Mark the Evangelist was a central figure in the promulgation of Christianity. Coulson (1958, 302) offers considerable skepticism about Mark's relics in a biographical sketch of the saint: "Under the high altar of San Marco in Venice lies, it is said, the body of the evangelist martyred in Alexandria, there venerated, and brought to San Marco by Venetian merchants in the ninth century. There is no reason to doubt the story's substance, though the identity of the piously stolen body depends on the solidarity of the Alexandrine tradition." That tradition is far from constituting proof.

The relics came to Venice in 829, whereupon construction of the Basilica di San Marco (St. Mark's Basilica) was begun immediately to enshrine them. In 1808 they were removed from their mausoleum beneath the altar flooring and are now kept in the high altar, surmounted by a green marble canopy resting on Greek columns carved with Gospel scenes (Cruz 1984, 117–18).

I visited San Marco's (see figure 2.3) with some Italian colleagues on October 11, 2004. After paying to see a collection of relics (including an alleged piece of the stone column of Jesus' flagellation) and paying again to stand in line to pass by St. Mark's reputed remains, I copied the inscription on the crypt (see figure 2.4): "CORPUS DIVI MARCI EVANGELISTAE" (Body of Divine [or Holy] Mark, Evangelist). On the reverse is "SALUTAT VOS . . . MARCUS FILIUS MEUS," annotated "1 Petri 5.13." This is an abridgement from the passage in 1 Peter 5:13: "The church that is at Babylon, elected together with you, saluteth you; and so doth Marcus my son."

Over the west door, as one is exiting San Marco's, is a lunette (a

Figure 2.3. St. Mark's Basilica in Venice boasts the remains of the author of the earliest Gospel (photo by author).

Figure 2.4. Crypt supposedly holding the relics of St. Mark (photo by author).

Figure 2.5. Lunette depicts St. Mark (right) and the Virgin standing on either side of the enthroned Christ (photo by author).

half-moon-shaped picture) depicting Christ between the Virgin and St. Mark, who presents his Gospel (see figure 2.5). In the adjoining piazzetta is a gray granite column with a sculpture of St. Mark's emblem—a winged lion, because he begins his Gospel by referring to the "wilderness" of which the lion is king (Coulson 1958, 302; Cruz 1984, 119).

The remaining Gospel writer, St. Luke, was apparently a physician and an early convert to Christianity. The genuineness of his relics has been disputed (Cruz 1984, 117):

> Little is known about the disposition of his relics until about the year 1463 when Padua and Venice both claimed to have the body of the saint and vied with one another over the authenticity of their relics. The bones in each place were eventually exhumed and carefully examined. Those at Venice were found to be the bones of a young man; those at Padua were of a man who died at a venerable age. Since the skull of the body in Padua was missing, and since the head was then known to be in Rome, the relics in Padua were accepted as being those of St. Luke. The Venetians were so disappointed in having their

relics pronounced invalid that they were vehement in their disapproval of the ecclesiastical pronouncement, so much so, that excommunication was threatened on all those who would continue to promote the relics in Venice as being valid. The relics have been enshrined in the Basilica of Santa Giustina above an altar in a side chapel. The tomb is of blue stone decorated with golden panels depicting portraits of angels, the saint and various symbols.

Of course, the head in Rome could have come from the skeleton at Padua without either of them being Luke's, especially given the lack of a historical record.

Among other disciples and early followers of Jesus were St. Paul (Saul of Tarsus), who is believed to have been beheaded in Rome. His head is supposedly preserved, along with that of St. Peter, in a golden urn in the Lateran. The Church of the Decapitation supposedly marks the site of his martyrdom. Its sanctuary houses the marble column to which he was supposedly bound, as well as the slab of marble on which he was executed. Also, "at the back of the church are three small buildings which protect the three miraculous fountains that are said to have bubbled forth when the head of St. Paul made three bounds on the slope" (Cruz 1984, 123).

Finally, there were the relics of Mary Magdalene, one of Jesus' inner circle of followers. At least three churches claimed to have her corpse (Meyer 1971, 73), while another had only her foot (Nickell 1998, 51). The monks of Vézelay claimed to have identified her tomb, and according to Coulson (1958, 324), "Thus the erection of one of the finest examples of Romanesque architecture was made possible by pilgrims to a spurious relic."

Later Saints

The relics of those who came after the contemporaries of Jesus but who were deemed worthy of veneration have also been zealously sought. For example, an entire cemetery was despoiled to provide one monastery with the relics of St. Ursula and her legendary eleven thousand virgin martyrs. An inscription from the fourth or fifth century told how a man led by visions had rebuilt a ruined Cologne basilica over the tomb of some virgin martyrs—without mention of dates, names, or numbers. However, explains Coulson (1958, 439):

> This is the nucleus of fact underlying preposterous elaborations of legend beginning in the ninth century. Ignorance of Latin epigraphy mistook eleven for 11,000, a mistake however which suggests that the martyrs were in fact eleven. Names were added, Ursula being taken from the tombstone of an eight year old girl of that name. At least as early as St. Dunstan, the Cologne martyrs were associated with Britain: the result, one might suggest, of confusing them with martyrs, probably nuns, who assisted the Anglo-Saxon mission to Germany and suffered death in the Low Countries. The excavation in the Twelfth Century of the cemetery surrounding the church of the Virgins provided relics of this multitude of martyrs. The identifications were supported by "revelations" supplying names and corroborative detail. . . .
>
> Thus took shape the legend of a British King's daughter visiting Rome with 11,000 virgins together with married associates and their children (to explain bones dug up in the cemetery) and their martyrdom on their return journey at the hands of the Huns, together with a non-existent Pope Cyriacus and equally non-existent bishops.

As one researcher commented regarding the relics of the alleged virgin martyrs, "The fact that many of these bones were unquestionably those of men did not affect their curative value" (Haggard 1929, 301).

The quest for relic acquisition led to further excesses. According to Meyer (1971, 73), "The living bodies of likely future saints were covetously watched by relic mongers; when Thomas Aquinas fell ill and died at a French monastery, his body was decapitated and his flesh boiled away by monks greedy for his bones." Moreover, "it is said that Saint Romuald of Ravenna heard during a visit to France that he was in mortal peril because of the value of his bones—he fled homeward, pretending to be mad."

Increasingly questionable Christian relics appeared. Teeth attributed to St. Apollonia (allegedly effective in curing toothaches) were too numerous to count, and a tooth of St. Peter was reputedly discovered resting on his tomb six hundred years after his death. There was also the gargantuan tooth of St. Paul, though some thought it might have belonged to "one of the monsters of the deep." Even though the relics of St. Paul, bishop of Leon, were reportedly burnt to powder during the Reformation, a nineteenth-century church somehow obtained his skull, the "entire bone of the right arm," and a finger, all kept in a silver reliquary (Nickell 1998, 50–51).

Among the macabre relics are the entire corpses of saints and other holy persons that have allegedly not succumbed to decay, even though the bodies were neither embalmed nor otherwise preserved. Study of such relics broaches the subjects of death and burial, disinterment, and preservation of bodies—topics that one credulous writer admits "would at first appear of morbid and macabre interest, but which eventually proved to be stimulating and fraught with mystery" (Cruz 1977, 21). The superstitious believe that incorruptibility is a sign of sanctity, proof of the miraculous, and evidence of God's endorsement of their religion.

Unfortunately, scientific evidence does not support such claims. In more than one instance of an "incorruptible" corpse, investigation has shown that the body had in fact been embalmed. For example, an examination of the corpse of St. Charles Borromeo (1538–1584) revealed that "the body of the Saint had been embalmed in the usual manner shortly after death," although "this was not held directly responsible for the preservation of the body almost three hundred years after the Saint's death." Yet one should keep in mind several additional facts: the body was never buried in the ground but in a tomb; its condition was monitored on several occasions, with new vestments and coffins provided; when it was found in a humid environment, it was removed until the condition was rectified; and it had been kept for three centuries in a presumably airtight reliquary under excellent environmental conditions (Cruz 1977, 190–93).

Another example is that of Philip Neri (1515–1595). Four years after he was interred above the first arch of the nave in a small chapel, his body was found "covered with cobwebs and dust," yet it was so well preserved as to be "undoubtedly miraculous," as attested by men of medicine. This case merely indicates the disposition to believe, even among physicians, at the time (or the peer pressure they felt to give credence to the miraculous). In fact, it has always been known that Philip's "viscera were removed and the body embalmed in a simple fashion after the Saint's autopsy in 1595." Also, a recent reference to the body's "last embalmment" suggests that the corpse had been repeatedly maintained (Cruz 1977, 210–12).

A "mysterious and delightful flower-like odor" is sometimes reported in cases of incorruptibility (Cruz 1977, 45, 48); this however, may be evidence of the use of an aromatic substance such as balsam, an oleoresin containing the preservative benzoic acid and commonly used for embalming (Nickell 1993, 86). The condition of many saints' corpses that have been pronounced incorruptible is actually unknown —or at least unreported in the standard text on the subject, Joan Carroll Cruz's *The Incorruptibles.* Among them is St. Alphege of Canterbury (954–1012), whose body was reportedly free of corruption in 1022, although its present state is not mentioned. Also, "no trace or relic remains" of St. Waltheof (d. 1159) to say whether the remains have been preserved (Cruz 1977, 64, 69–70).

Some relics must be classified as, at best, *formerly* incorruptible. For instance, the body of St. Edward the Confessor (1004–1066) was exhumed thirty-six years after his death and found to be incorrupt; when the coffin was opened in 1685, the remains were completely skeletonized. When the body of St. Agnes of Montepulciano (1268–1317) was placed inside the walls of the church's main altar, the tomb was excessively humid, and the body decomposed (Nickell 1993, 88).

Many "incorruptible" bodies are more accurately described as mummified; that is, the body is desiccated—a state that can occur naturally under certain conditions (such as being kept in a dry tomb or catacombs) or can be induced by embalming. For instance, the body of St. Urbald of Gubbio (circa 1100–1160) was officially examined in 1960 and found to be mummified, having skin like brown leather (Nickell 1993, 89).

But what about cases in which the corpse has been discovered intact despite perpetually wet conditions? As forensic pathologists and anthropologists know, a body that has been submerged in water or wet soil for a long time may form a soaplike substance called adipocere (popularly known as "grave wax"). Depending on the subsequent conditions, the body may eventually take on the leathery effect of mummification or decompose completely (Ubelaker and Scammell 1992, 150–51; Geberth 1993, 571–72).

In many cases, artificial means have been used to help preserve a corpse or to conceal its poor condition. Consider, for example, the caption of the cover photograph of *The Incorruptibles,* which reads: "The incorruptible body of Saint Bernadette Soubirous of Lourdes, France (1844–1879), preserved intact for 100 years without embalming or other artificial means." It would take an autopsy by independent authorities to determine whether (as happened in other cases) St. Bernadette's corpse had actually been given injections of embalming fluid. But in any event, when Bernadette's body was first exhumed, thirty years after her death, it was found to be "emaciated" —probably in the early stages of mummification. Significantly, the perfect appearance of her face and hands, as shown in photographs, is due to their being covered with wax and sculpted in the manner of Madame Tussaud's famous museum figures (Nickell 1993, 90–92; Cruz 1984, 218–20).

An alleged preservation of another kind involves the "blood" of the legendary martyr San Gennaro—St. Januarius—who was supposedly the bishop of Benevento, Italy, when he was beheaded during the persecution of Christians by Diocletian (Roman emperor 284–305). According to a pious tale, after lions refused to harm Januarius and his companions, they were cast into a fiery furnace but remained uninjured. Finally, they were beheaded at Pozzuoli, and two vials of Januarius' blood were taken with his remains to the Neopolitan catacombs. The reputed relics were disinterred in the fifth century, housed in various locales over the next several centuries, and permanently enshrined in a Naples cathedral in the latter thirteenth century. (See figure 2.6.)

As eyewitnesses dating back to at least the fourteenth century have reported, the substance that is purportedly the martyred saint's

Figure 2.6. Legendary St. Januarius, holding two vials of his own blood, is portrayed in this souvenir figure from Naples (author's collection; photo by author).

congealed blood periodically liquefies, reddens, and froths—in an apparent contravention of natural laws. The "blood" half fills a pear-shaped ampoule; a narrow, adjacent vial is now essentially empty, its contents supposedly dispensed to wealthy families in the eighteenth century. The vials are mounted in a cylindrical silver case that has clear glass faces for viewing, as well as a handle by which it can be held or fitted into an ornate monstrance. A ritual takes place several times annually, during which a priest exposes the congealed blood before another reliquary, a bust that is supposed to contain the martyr's skull (but which apparently contains only small bone fragments). According to tradition, if the phenomenon fails to occur, disaster is imminent (Nickell and Fischer 1992, 145–51).

Reasons for suspicion abound. First, the Catholic Church has never been able to verify the historical existence of San Gennaro. No contemporary reference to him has been discovered, nor does his name appear in any of the early Roman martyrologies. Moreover, there is absolutely no record of the saint's blood relics prior to 1389, when an unknown traveler reported his astonishment at witnessing the liquefaction. And the legend of their acquisition—that Januarius' nurse was present at his beheading and obtained some of his blood in two vials that were then placed in his funeral urn—is as improbable as it is modern. The legend dates from the sixteenth century, some two hundred years after the vials appeared in Naples.

Another reason for suspicion is that the blood of some twenty additional saints is said to liquefy, and virtually all these relics are found in the Naples area. This seems to suggest some regional secret, rather than the miraculous. It is important to note that no sustained scientific scrutiny of the blood relics has ever been permitted. Also, descriptions of the liquefaction vary, and it is not always easy to determine what may be permutations in the phenomenon's occurrence or differences attributable to individual perceptions. Assertions that the substance in the vials is genuine blood are based solely on spectroscopic analyses using antiquated equipment under poor conditions, casting grave doubts on the results. The researchers themselves admitted that certain dyes can be mistaken for hemoglobin. (For a full discussion of the Januarian legend and phenomena, see Nickell and Fischer 1992, 145–64).

Various hypotheses have been offered to account for the liquefaction, including the idea that real blood was preserved with resin or wax or that it involved a concoction of blood and chalk; an aqueous suspension of chocolate powder, casein, and other ingredients; a mixture of tallow, ether, and carmine; or some other recipe. Not surprisingly, there were problems of homogeneity, historical availability, and the probable effects of age. Forensic analyst John F. Fischer and I offered our own solution to the phenomenon, involving a mixture of olive oil, melted beeswax, and pigment. Only a small amount of wax is added, so that the mixture is solid when cool, but when it is slightly warmed (by body heat, candles, or the like), the trace of congealing substance melts, and the mixture liquefies. As one authority states,

"A very important fact is that liquefaction has occurred during repair of the casket, a circumstance in which it seems highly unlikely that God would work a miracle" (Coulson 1958, 239).

In 1991, before we could publish our research, a team of Italian scientists made international headlines with their own solution to the Januarian mystery. Writing in the journal *Nature*, Professor Luigi Garlaschelli (Department of Organic Chemistry, University of Pavia) and two colleagues from Milan, Franco Ramaccini and Sergio Della Sala, proposed "that thixotropy may furnish an explanation." A thixotropic gel becomes fluid when agitated and resolidifies when allowed to stand. The Italian scientists created such a gel by mixing chalk and hydrated iron chloride with a small amount of salt water and reported a convincing replication of the Januarian phenomenon (Garlaschelli et al. 1991). In 1996 Garlaschelli was able to examine a similar liquefying blood relic, that of St. Lorenzo at the Church of St. Maria in Arnaseno, Italy. Using a test-tube mixer, he whirled the ampoule containing the "blood" to test the thixotropic gel hypothesis, but there was no effect. He then immersed the ampoule in warm water, whereupon a "miracle" occurred: the contents melted and turned red—just like the Januarian phenomenon (Polidoro 2004a).

In 2004, along with Luigi Garlaschelli himself, I visited the four Italian sites that hold the reputed relics of San Gennaro, and we discussed all the evidence. The first site, the Chapel of the Treasury, is situated inside the Cathedral of Naples (see figure 2.7). This baroque chapel—rich in frescoes and marbles—holds the gilded silver bust of the saint and the ampoule of "blood" that periodically liquefies and then coagulates. Garlaschelli (2004) cautions that the St. Januarius and St. Lorenzo "blood" relics do not necessarily work on the same principle; he still believes that the former may be a thixotropic substance.

The Museum of San Gennaro's Treasury, which is adjacent to the cathedral, holds seven centuries' worth of artworks and treasures that were donated to the saint but were not placed on exhibition until relatively recently. The Spire of San Gennaro, located a short distance from the cathedral, is an impressive monument, twenty-four

Figure 2.7. A gilded bust of St. Januarius, portrayed as a bishop, contains his alleged relics (photo by author).

Figure 2.8. Investigator Luigi Garlaschelli poses with the Pozzuoli Stone on which St. Januarius was legendarily beheaded (photo by author).

meters high. It was commissioned in 1636 by the Deputation of San Gennaro's Treasure in gratitude for the saint's supposed protection, five years earlier, against the eruption of nearby Mount Vesuvius.

The Church of Capuchin Monks at Pozzuoli is just a short train ride from Naples. It contains the marble slab, installed in the church wall, reputed to be the stone on which Januarius was beheaded (see figure 2.8). In the late 1980s, however, the stone was examined and determined to be a paleo-Christian altar, possibly dating from the seventh century (hundreds of years after the martyrdom). The red spots that were supposed to be blood are believed to be traces from an old painting, along with some candle drippings. According to Garlaschelli (2004), the church itself now discourages the cult of the Pozzuoli Stone "as a superstition originating from the wishful thinking and self-delusion of the worshippers."

CHAPTER 3

The Holy Grail

For centuries, romantic stories about the quest for the *San Grèal* or Holy Grail—popularly believed to be the cup used by Christ at the Last Supper (see figure 3.1)—have proliferated. Here I examine the Grail legends, the historical evidence, the Grail as relic, and *The Da Vinci Code,* the best-selling novel that sparked a revival of interest in the Grail.

Grail Legends

Popularly, the Holy Grail is the talisman sought by the knights of King Arthur's Round Table. The quest is known to English audiences largely through a compilation and translation of French romances by Sir Thomas Malory. Completed by 1470, Malory's *Morte d'Arthur* represents the Grail as the chalice Jesus and his disciples drank from at the Last Supper and that was subsequently used to catch and preserve his blood from the Crucifixion. The latter act was usually attributed to Mary Magdalene or Joseph of Arimathea; it was Joseph who approached Pilate to request Jesus' body for burial (Mark 15:43–46). A legend claimed that Joseph took the cup to Britain.

It appears that, originally, the word *grail* meant "dish." For example, one early French text speaks of "boars' heads on grails of silver." In fact, the first Christian Grail story, penned by Robert de

Figure 3.1. The Holy Grail—popularly, the chalice from the Last Supper—is sometimes associated with the suit of cups in the tarot deck (author's collection).

Boron, presents it as a dish on which the Passover lamb had been served at the Last Supper.

The earliest Grail romance, *Le Conte du Graal* (The Story of the Grail), was composed in about 1190 by Chrétien de Troyes. It introduced Perceval, a guileless knight and an archetypal fool in the Grail romances. At a feast at the castle of the Fisher King (a mysterious character who appears in various Arthurian and Grail legends), Perceval first encounters what he believes is the Grail. As Chrétien relates (quoted and translated in Barber 2004, 17–18):

> While they were talking of one thing and another, a boy came from a
> chamber clutching a white lance by the middle of the shaft, and
> passed between the fire and the two who were sitting on the bed.
> Everyone in the hall saw the white lance with its white head; and a

drop of blood issued from the tip of the lance's head, and right down to the boy's hand this red drop ran. The lord's guest gazed at this marvel that had appeared there that night, but restrained himself from asking how it came to be, because he remembered the advice of the nobleman who made him a knight, who taught and instructed him to beware of talking too much; he feared it would be considered base of him if he asked, so he did not. Just then two other boys appeared, and in their hands they held candlesticks of the finest gold, inlaid with black enamel. The boys who carried the candlesticks were handsome indeed. In each candlestick burned ten candles at the very least. A girl who came in with the boys, fair and comely and beautifully adorned, was holding a grail between her hands. When she entered holding the grail, so brilliant a light appeared that the candles lost their brightness like the stars or the moon when the sun rises. After her came another girl, holding a silver trencher. The grail, which went ahead, was made of fine, pure gold; and in it were precious stones of many kinds, the richest and most precious in the earth or the sea: those in the grail surpassed all other jewels without a doubt. They passed before the bed as the lance had done, and disappeared into another chamber. The boy saw them pass, but did not dare to ask who was served from the grail, for he had taken the words of the wise nobleman to heart. I fear he may suffer for doing so, for I have heard it said that in time of need a man can talk too little as well as too much. I don't know whether it will bring him good or ill, but he asked nothing.

This "is the original of all subsequent descriptions of the Grail and its surroundings" (Barber 2004, 19).

Two other Grail stories, both written by Robert de Boron in about 1200, were *Joseph d'Arimathie* and *Merlin*. These gave the quest for the Holy Grail a new Christian focus, representing it as a spiritual rather than a chivalrous search. Subsequently, the latest of the French Grail romances, the *Quête del Saint Graal* (Quest of the Holy Grail), served as the basis for Malory's *Morte d'Arthur*. This epic represents the most important and best-known English version of the Arthurian and Grail adventures (Cox 2004, 75–76). (Much later, the story was also told by Tennyson in his *Idylls of the King*.) By the time of Malory's *Morte d'Arthur*, the Grail story had become a thoroughly Christian one—a tale concerning spirituality and repentance. It was not, however, orthodox Christianity, since Galahad's quest occurred independently of the church (Duchane 2004, 77–78).

In the various legends, the Holy Grail has been represented as a silver platter, a crystal vase filled with blood, a miraculous cauldron or dish of plenty, and a salver bearing a man's severed head (like that of John the Baptist in Matthew 14:3–12), among other depictions. About 1205 a Bavarian poem, *Parzival,* written by Wolfram von Eschenbach, first represented the Grail as something other than a dish or cup. It was instead described as a magical, luminous stone (Cox 2004, 76). A princess carried this "perfection of Paradise," this "thing that was called the Grail, earth's perfection's transcendence" (quoted and translated in Barber 2004, 174). Later in the poem the Grail is described more specifically as an emerald from Lucifer's crown, having fallen to earth during the struggle in heaven (Ralls 2004, 50). Over time, the Grail has also been portrayed as a reliquary containing the sacred Host or the precious blood of Christ, a sculpted head of Jesus, a fish, a dove, a sword, a lance, a secret book, manna from heaven, a table, a beatific vision, the philosopher's stone, and many other representations (Cox 2004, 74–75; Duchane 2004, 9; Ralls 2004, 49; *Encyclopaedia Britannica* 1960, s.v. "Grail, the Holy").

In medieval texts, the Grail is fundamentally a mystery, an inner knowing that is difficult to reduce to words. Because some of the stories had themes and details related to the famous Knights Templar, an order of military monks, a legend has gown up that the Templars were guardians of the secret spiritual tradition (see figure 3.2). The Rosicrucians and Freemasons also had mystical Grail traditions (Ralls 2004, 47; Duchane 2004, 23–26; Barber 2004, 360).

Indeed, the mystery of the Grail continues to evolve, as I explore later in the section on *The Da Vinci Code.* The term *Holy Grail* is now popularly used to refer to any object of a quest, usually an unattainable one.

Historical Evidence

Despite the emotive power and the proliferation of legends about the Grail, the idea of a Christian origin of the legend lacks scholarly credibility. No story about Joseph of Arimathea and the Holy Grail exists in any text until the end of the twelfth century, when Robert de Bo-

Figure 3.2. The Knights Templar were an order of military monks; shown (left to right) are an armed and mounted knight, a grand master of the order, and a knight wearing his domestic robes (from *Proctor's History of the Crusades*).

ron penned his romance. Notably, the Gospel accounts of Jesus' death give no justification to the notion that Joseph or anyone else obtained a dish or chalice from the Last Supper and used it or any other receptacle to preserve Jesus' blood. All four narratives of the Passion mention Joseph (Matthew 27:57–60; Mark 15:43–46; Luke 23:50–53; and John 19:38–40), but not until after Jesus dies on the cross; Joseph is not mentioned again after Jesus' body has been interred.

The pious legend that Joseph took the Grail to England's Glastonbury Abbey is of very late vintage. In the twelfth century, that story was unknown to the chronicler of the period, William of Malmesbury. In the next century, however, possibly influenced by the Grail romances, a tale of Joseph playing a prominent role in the abbey's foundation appeared in a new edition of William's work. Subsequently, a mid-fourteenth-century history of the abbey, written by John of Glastonbury, actually utilized the Grail romances as source material

(Barber 2004, 131). The story was elaborated at the end of the fifteenth century when Glastonbury's abbot, Richard Bere, promoted the cult of St. Joseph of Glastonbury and accordingly revamped the abbey's coat of arms. Reports Barber (2004, 133–34):

> Until then, there had been a tradition that Joseph was buried in the old church, which had burned down in 1184, and that he had brought two cruets containing the blood and sweat of Our Lord to the abbey, where they had been hidden. This was attributed to an otherwise unknown writer called Melkin, who prophesied that when Joseph's body was found, "it will be visible, whole and undecayed, and open to the whole world." The first mention of this prophecy is in John of Glastonbury's chronicle. But, despite its huge political potential—if Joseph was the founder of Glastonbury, the abbey would claim to be on par with Rome, as an apostolic foundation—the idea was never developed. The English rulers had encouraged the monks to search for Arthur's remains in the 1180s, and twice in the succeeding centuries, royal initiatives were launched to find Joseph of Arimathea's tomb. We know little more about the first such attempt than that Edward III encouraged a mystic to seek the grave in 1345. In 1419 Henry V, wishing to emphasize the independence of the English church, encouraged the monks to excavate in search of Joseph of Arimathea's tomb. A carefully worded report, from which the king might infer that Joseph's body had been found, even though the abbot did not say so directly, was sent back. But it seems that the death of Henry V, and the end of the gathering of ecclesiastics, the Council of Constance, at which the claim that the English church had been founded by Joseph was of great importance, led to the abandonment of this attempt to establish the legend. The abbey was remarkably reticent about a story which had the potential to make it one of the great shrines of Christendom, and Glastonbury never claimed to have the Grail.

"Ironically," continues Barber, "it was only in Protestant England that a relic said to be the Grail was given a Glastonbury provenance." (The various competing Grail chalices are discussed later in this chapter.)

Like the legend of Joseph at Glastonbury, records relating to relics of the Holy Blood—the supposed contents of the cup that Joseph of Arimathea possessed—are of equally late date. Perhaps the earliest comes from Mantra, Italy, where such a relic was found—according to a contemporary chronicle—in 804. Other relics of the Holy Blood, including that of Bruges, Belgium, are even more recent (see chapter 11) (Barber 2004, 128–31).

Writings aside, there were, however, early visual images of the Crucifixion depicting a chalice in which Christ's blood was collected from his pierced side. But even these date from the ninth century and after. Earlier pictures show a chalice at the foot of the cross, but this may be only the container of vinegar given to Jesus to drink (Mark 15:36; Barber 2004, 120).

There is no provenance for any Holy Grail chalice or its contents until centuries after the Crucifixion, and there is no first-century evidence as to what happened to either of them or to Joseph of Arimathea, "assuming he's even an historical character," comments Eric Eve, a New Testament scholar at Oxford University. He adds, "The probability that the cup found its way to Joseph and that he traveled with it to Britain is as near as nil as makes no difference. I would say it is purely legendary" (quoted in O'Neill 2004). Others agree. Richard Barber observes that the Grail legend originated more than a millennium after the death of Jesus, imagined by Chrétien de Troyes. Noting that Chrétien's vision is the source of all Grail stories, he says of the legend, "It is pure literature" (quoted in O'Neill 2004).

Another skeptic is Richard Holloway, former bishop of Edinburgh, who says, "It's all good fun but absolute nonsense." He adds, "The quest for the Holy Grail belongs with the quest for the ark Noah left on Mount Ararat or the fabled Ark of the Covenant Indiana Jones is always chasing. There ain't any objective truth in any of it—but of course it's a dream for publishers who know the world is full of gullible people looking for miracles and they keep on promising that this time the miracle's going to come true." Holloway concludes, "Only it isn't—but the money keeps rolling in" (quoted in O'Neill 2004).

The Grail as Relic

Several vessels lay claim to being the authentic Holy Grail—that is, a chalice or dish from the Last Supper, a vessel that contained Christ's blood from the Crucifixion, or both. Some twenty vessels claiming

Figure 3.3. Statue of Faith holding the Holy Grail stands before the Gran Madre di Dio church in Turin. According to local legend, this is the site where the Holy Grail is hidden (photo by author).

the title Holy Grail had surfaced by the sixteenth century, since Grails, like other venerated relics—genuine or not—were a source of both pride and income to the church, the monastery, or the city that had them. (See figure 3.3.) According to an article in *Catholic Digest*, "careful examination and tracking of documents, however, reduced that number to eight by the 18th century, and further research eventually rejected most other claims." One, for instance, was merely "a very old platter that might have held a cooked lamb at a Passover meal," while another, from Jerusalem, was apparently a "wine jar" (McGuire 1999, 10).

Some believed that the Marian Chalice was the Grail. St. Helena, the mother of emperor Constantine the Great of Constantinople, allegedly "discovered" many sensational relics on a pilgrimage to Palestine in about A.D. 326. In addition to the True Cross (the subject of chapter 5), she supposedly found a chalice during the excavation of a tomb that she believed to be Jesus'. Helena is said to have concluded that it was the cup from the Last Supper used by Mary Magdalene to collect Jesus' blood. It was thus named the Marian Chalice

(Duchane 2004, 48–51). Unfortunately, the accounts of Helena's alleged discoveries date from a much later period than the reputed excavations; they do not appear until the end of the fourth century, and then only in the West (*Encyclopaedia Britannica* 1960, s.v. "Helena, St."). In any event, the Marian Chalice was reportedly taken to Rome and then to Britain for protection when Rome was invaded by the Visigoths in 410. It has been variously described as a small stone cup or a larger silver one, or as the original cup contained in a larger gold vessel decorated with jewels. Its whereabouts are no longer known (Duchane 2004, 51).

Among the existing "Grails," some are centuries-old Catholic relics, and others are new candidates put forward since the latter nineteenth century. Here is a brief look at several of them. (Except as otherwise noted, information is from Barber 2004, 167–72, 297–302; and Cruz 1984, 27–30.) Among the earliest purported Grails is one at Genoa, known as *il sacro catino* (the sacred bowl). Tradition says that it was carved from a great emerald—it is some eighteen inches across—but it is actually a hexagonal Egyptian dish of green glass. As William of Tyre wrote in about 1170, it was taken as booty from the mosque at Caesarea during the First Crusade in 1101: "In this same chapel was found a vase of brilliant green shaped like a bowl. The Genoese, believing that it was of emerald, took it in lieu of a large sum of money and thus acquired a splendid ornament for their church. They still show this vase as a marvel to people of distinction who pass through their city, and persuade them to believe it is truly an emerald, as its color indicates." A different version reports that it was booty taken from Almeria, Spain, in 1147. However, not until the end of the thirteenth century was the bowl equated with the Grail.

Rivaling the Genoa vessel is the *santo caliz* (holy chalice) of the Cathedral of Valencia, Spain. It is a simple carnelian cup in a medieval mount of gold studded with pearls and gems. It is claimed to be the only one of the various reputed Grails "to have survived intense investigation and skepticism" (McGuire 1999, 7). In fact, however, the earliest undisputed reference to the chalice is from 1399, when

Figure 3.4. The Antioch chalice is one of several cups touted as the Holy Grail (photo from an old leaflet, collection of Center for Inquiry Libraries, Amherst, N.Y.).

the monastery of San Juan de la Peña traded it to the king of Aragon for a gold cup.

Of much more recent discovery is a plain silver cup mounted in an ornate outer chalice. It was found in Syria in 1910 as part of a cache of altar vessels uncovered in an ancient dry well—probably hidden there for safekeeping during an invasion. Now enshrined in the Metropolitan Museum of Art in New York City, the chalice is intricately carved with more than 240 designs, including a figure of Christ on either side. Those who believe that it is the Holy Grail speculate that it accompanied Saul and Barnabas when they journeyed to Antioch (present-day Antakya, Turkey), as related in the Acts of the Apostles (11:25–26). However, the museum cautions: "The identification of the 'Antioch Chalice' as the Holy Grail has not been sustained, and its authenticity has even been challenged, but the work has usually been considered a sixth-century chalice meant to be used in the Eucharist." Moreover, "most recently its shape has been recognized as more closely resembling sixth-century standing lamps, its decoration possibly in recognition of Christ's words 'I am the light of the world' (John 8:12)" (Antioch chalice 2005). (See figure 3.4.)

Another Antioch cup was discovered in the 1930s in a cave outside that city. It is a stemmed Roman glass bowl, and an advertisement for its London exhibition declared it to be "The Holy Grail." However, in 1935 the editor of *Antiquity* challenged that claim: "We should be glad to be told exactly how the advertiser knows that the 'newly discovered cup' is the Holy Grail" (quoted in Barber 2004, 300). Skeptics are still waiting for that information.

Two other Grails came from the British Isles. One was "discovered" at Glastonbury Abbey in 1906 after having been concealed there a few years earlier. Antiquarians concluded that it was probably not ancient. The other rivaled the Glastonbury Grail after it came to light in Wales. It has since been shown to be a late-medieval elmwood mazer (a large drinking bowl) such as that used in monasteries.

A recent Grail claim is featured in *The Chalice of Magdalene* by Graham Phillips (2004). Of uncertain date, it has no meaningful provenance. One source describes the discovery as "a small Roman onyx scent jar" (Ford 2005).

As these examples demonstrate, there is no credible evidence that a vessel from the Last Supper was preserved. Moreover, observes Barber (2004, 170), "there is little or no evidence that anyone claimed in the thirteenth century to possess the Grail." All the alleged Grail vessels date from after the period when most of the Grail romances were penned—between 1190 and 1240.

But what if the Grail is not an actual object but rather a metaphor for a secret handed down through history by a select few? That is the central concept in the popular novel *The Da Vinci Code.*

The Da Vinci Hoax

Dan Brown's best-selling *The Da Vinci Code* (2003) has led to renewed interest in the Grail quest, restyling the legend for a public that often gorges itself on a diet of pseudoscience, pseudohistory, and fantasy. (See figure 3.5.) The adventure tale begins with Paris police summoning Robert Langdon, an Indiana Jones type, to the Louvre to view the corpse of curator Jacques Saunière, who has been murdered in bizarre circumstances. A bloody star, an ancient pentacle, appears

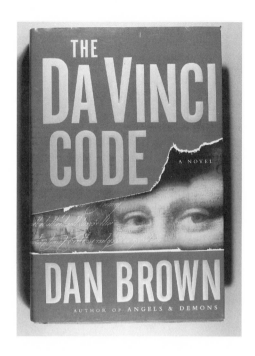

Figure 3.5. The novel *The Da Vinci Code* is based on the quest for the Holy Grail (author's collection).

on his abdomen, painted by himself in his own blood. Also, with an invisible-ink felt marker (used by museum staff to secretly mark items), he has scrawled a cryptic message on the parquet floor beside him, discovered by forensic technicians wielding black lights.

Soon Langdon and beautiful cryptanalyst Sophie Neveu lead readers on a page-turning treasure hunt across France and England, propelled by a series of puzzles and clues that eventually end at Scotland's Rosslyn Chapel. Reported one critic, "Several corpses later in this twenty-first-century retelling of the Holy Grail legend, the murders are solved. But the final resting place of the Grail comes only in the Epilogue, in an oh-yes-I-forgot-to-tell-you finale: Dan Brown has led his readers on a classic wild goose chase" (Bernstein 2004, 7).

Along the way, Brown's hero and heroine search for a hidden "truth" that challenges mainstream Christianity. Brown drew heavily on the best seller *Holy Blood, Holy Grail*, written by Michael Baigent, Richard Leigh, and Henry Lincoln (1996), with Lincoln as the conceptual author. Brown's novel is predicated on a conspiracy theory involving Jesus and Mary Magdalene. Supposedly the old

Figure 3.6. Statue of
Leonardo da Vinci in Milan
(photo by author).

French word *sangreal* can be explained not as *san greal* (holy grail)
but as *sang real* (royal blood). Although that concept was not current
before the late Middle Ages, according to the *Catholic Encyclopedia*
(1909, s.v. "The Holy Grail"), *Holy Blood, Holy Grail* argues that
Jesus was married to Mary Magdalene, that they had a child, and
even that he may have survived the Crucifixion. Jesus' child, or so
the "nonfiction" book claims, thus began a bloodline that led to the
Merovingian dynasty, a succession of kings who ruled present-day
France from 481 to 751. Evidence of the holy bloodline was supposedly found in a trove of parchment documents discovered by Bérenger
Saunière, the priest of Rennes-le-Château in the Pyrenees. The secret
had been kept by a shadowy society known as the Priory of Sion,
which harked back to the era of the Knights Templar and claimed
among its past grand masters Leonardo da Vinci (see figure 3.6), Isaac
Newton, and Victor Hugo.

Brown seizes on Leonardo, borrowing from "The Secret Code of Leonardo Da Vinci," a chapter of another work of pseudohistory titled *The Templar Revelation,* coauthored by "researchers" Lynn Picknett and Clive Prince (1998). Their previous foray into nonsense was their claim that Leonardo had created the Shroud of Turin, despite the fact that the shroud appeared nearly a century before the great artist and inventive genius was even born (see chapter 9). Among the "revelations" of Picknett and Prince adopted by Brown in *The Da Vinci Code* is the claim that Leonardo's fresco *The Last Supper* contains hidden symbolism relating to the *sang real* secret. They claim, for instance, that St. John in the picture (seated at the right of Jesus) is actually a woman—Mary Magdalene—and that the shape made by "Mary" and Jesus is "a giant, spreadeagled 'M,' almost as if they were literally joined at the hip but had suffered a falling out or even grown apart" (Picknett and Prince 1998, 19–21). By repeating this silliness, Brown provokes one critic to note that his characterizations "bear little resemblance to the serious thinking in the field" of Leonardo studies and reveal "a stunning lack of careful knowledge" about his subject (Bernstein 2004, 12). Brown combines such elements to portray Mary Magdalene (see figure 3.7) as the representative of the goddess concept, embodied in early Christianity. Janet Maslin of the *New York Times* understands the "entire story" of *The Da Vinci Code* "as a hunt for the Lost Sacred Feminine essence" (quoted in Burstein 2004, 75).

Alas, the whole basis of *The Da Vinci Code*—the parchments of Rennes-le-Château and the Priory of Sion—"were conclusively proven in the 1990s to have been part of an elaborate hoax" (Bernstein 2004, 9). This hoax has been attributed to a man named Pierre Plantard (Olson and Miesel 2004, 223–39). Investigative writer Massimo Polidoro (2004b, 24) of Milan writes:

> Plantard was an anti-Semite and the leader of a minor occult, right-wing organization known as Alpha Galates. His scheme was quite ingenious and complex. He had the parchments made by an artist friend, Philippe de Cherisey; then, he passed them on as real to Gérard de Sède, to whom he also told the invented story of Saunière's findings.

Figure 3.7. Purported relics of Mary Magdalene from Turin's Church of Maria Ausiliatrice include (from top) hair, bones, and a piece of her vest (photo by Stefano Bagnasco).

> Plantard also invented the Priory of Sion in 1956 and created fake
> manuscripts and documents that linked the Priory to [Rennes-le-
> Château] and deposited them at the National Library in Paris, where
> he suggested Lincoln and friends [authors of *Holy Blood, Holy Grail*]
> go to look for important discoveries.

The hoax snookered not only the authors of *Holy Blood, Holy Grail*
but also Picknett and Prince, who asserted that "the *Dossiers secrets*,"
the bogus Priory of Sion documents, "may appear to be complete nonsense, but the sheer scale of the effort and resources put into them, and
into maintaining their claims, gives one pause." They continued, "The
mass of evidence assembled by Baigent, Leigh and Lincoln for the historical existence of the Priory is unassailable" (Picknett and Prince
1998, 45, 48).

Picknett and Prince have since changed their tune—sort of. They
now admit that they were wrong yet strive to convince readers that
they were somehow right after all. They blithely state: "The conclusion that we've come to since writing *The Templar Revelation* is
that the Priory of Sion that declared itself to the world in 1956 was
invented then, but as a front for a network of related secret societies
and esoteric orders that do have a genuine pedigree. There's a close
connection between the modern Priory of Sion and secret societies
that claim descent from the medieval Templars. . . . The network of
orders behind the Priory of Sion is closely intertwined with certain
forms of Freemasonry, such as the Rectified Scottish Rite" (*Secrets*
2004, 66).

Of course, Brown was also duped by the Priory of Sion hoax, but
he "remains unrepentant," according to Bernstein (2004, 15). And his
apologists point out that *The Da Vinci Code* is, after all, fiction. Nevertheless, he assured readers at the beginning of the novel, under the
heading "Fact," that "the Priory of Sion—a European secret society
founded in 1099—is a real organization" (Brown 2003, 1).

Despite the devastatingly negative evidence, *The Da Vinci Code*
mania continues. Angered by the novel's treatment of Leonardo,
Alessandro Vezzosi, an Italian museum director, joined with art experts and clerics to hold a "trial" to establish the truth about the

novel. "Leonardo is misrepresented and belittled," Vezzosi stated. "His importance is misunderstood." The mock trial's speakers pointed out numerous errors and misconceptions fostered by Brown (Falconi 2005). A thorough debunking is *The Da Vinci Hoax: Exposing the Errors in* The Da Vinci Code (Olson and Miesel 2004). Perhaps Brown should go on his own quest—for the truth.

CHAPTER 4

Self-Portraits of Jesus

Since the beginning of Christianity, the question of Jesus' physical appearance has provoked an almost Grail-like quest. There are legends—and pictures to go with them—that Jesus miraculously provided his own self-portrait. Here I investigate the earliest concepts of Jesus' likeness, his purportedly miraculous Edessan image, and the face he legendarily imprinted on Veronica's Veil.

The Likeness of Jesus

No clue to the physical appearance of Jesus exists in the Gospels, the Epistles, or anywhere in the New Testament, the Apocrypha, or contemporary histories. As St. Augustine lamented in the early fifth century, although there were many representations of Christ, "we do not know of his external appearance, nor that of his mother." Despite Jesus' representation on the Shroud of Turin as tall, bearded, and impressive in appearance, he may have been none of those things. Indeed, in an Old Testament prophecy of the coming of the Messiah, Isaiah wrote:

> He hath no form nor comeliness; and when we see him, there is no beauty that we should desire him.
> He is despised and rejected of men; a man of sorrows, and acquainted with grief: and we hid as it were our faces from him; he was despised, and we esteemed him not. (Isaiah 53:2–3)

Consequently, many early Christian writers thought Christ ugly; others, however, argued that Isaiah was surely referring to the appearance of the crucified Jesus, and they cited another passage they believed to be prophetic: "Thou art fairer than the children of men; grace is poured into thy lips; therefore God hath blessed thee for ever" (Psalms 45:2).

Given such disparate, putative prophecies and a lack of any biblical description, it is not surprising that we find varying conceptual portraits of Jesus from the early centuries. Another factor that may have played a part is the Judaic prohibition against graven images: "Thou shalt not make unto thee any graven image, or any likeness of any thing that is in heaven above, or that is in the earth beneath, or that is in the water under the earth. Thou shalt not bow down thyself to them" (Exodus 20:4–5). Because this prohibition seems to have carried over into early Christianity, it may help to explain the paucity of Christ images.

Although attempts were made to produce portraits or other painted images of Jesus, none are known until long after his death. The earliest representation is from the middle of the third century; this painting, done in fresco, depicts him as young, beardless, and with cropped hair. There are other similar representations. States David Sox (1978, 51), "The earliest portrayals of Jesus in Christian art were generally of an Apollo or young shepherd type." This type of portrayal—images that were idealistic, "almost ethereal," rather than realistic—continued into the fourth and fifth centuries. They were expressions of faith and of Christian piety (Adams 1972, 8).

However, beginning in the third and fourth centuries, the Apollo-type Christ image was paralleled by a more Semitic representation with long, flowing hair and beard; large, accentuated eyes; and a prominent nose. Eventually this concept prevailed—throughout the Byzantine Empire and later in Europe—as a matter of rigid artistic convention. According to Marcello Craveri in *The Life of Jesus* (1967, 163):

> To explain how after so many centuries it was possible to make an authentic portrait of the Savior, it was said that there had always been

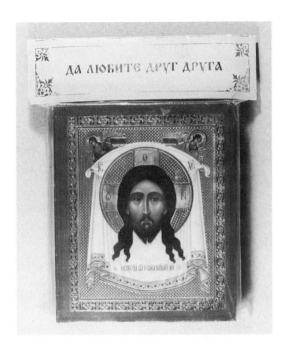

ДА ЛЮБИТЕ ДРУГ ДРУГА

Figure 4.1. Icon of the face of Christ imprinted on cloth derives from proliferating legends (souvenir from Moscow, author's collection).

a traditional secret picture composed by none other than Luke. The first to tell of this legend was Andrew, metropolitan of Crete, in 710. Backed up by such contentions, portraits of Jesus multiplied to such an extent that only a few years later Emperor Leo III the Isaurian had to order a harsh persecution against images, which led to passionate debates on the legitimacy of portraying Jesus and the danger of falling into heathen idolatry.

The Image of Edessa

As early as the sixth century, there also appeared certain images of Jesus that were reputed to be *acheiropoietos,* or "not made with hands" (Humber 1978, 83; Wilson 1979, 112). There were several of these, and as many legends to account for their supposedly miraculous origin (see figure 4.1).

Among the legends is one concerning the image of Edessa. The story is related in a mid-fourth-century Syriac manuscript, *The Doctrine of Addai,* which tells how a leprosy-afflicted King Abgar of Edessa (now Urfa, in south-central Turkey) supposedly sent a messenger named Ananias to deliver a letter to Jesus. The text of this reputed letter was included in an official history of the Edessan image written soon after the cloth was transferred from Edessa to Constantinople (see Wilson 1979, 272–90). In the letter, Abgar sends "greetings to Jesus the Savior who has come to light as a good physician in the city of Jerusalem" and who, he has heard, "can make the blind see, the lame walk . . . heal those who are tortured by chronic illnesses, and . . . raise the dead." Abgar believes that Jesus is either God himself or the Son of God, so he entreats Jesus to "come to me and cure me of my disease." He notes that he has heard of the Jews' plan to harm Jesus and adds, "I have a very small city, but it is stately and will be sufficient for us both to live in peace."

According to the tale, Abgar instructs Ananias that if he is unable to persuade Jesus to return with him to Edessa, he should bring back a portrait instead. But while Ananias is sitting on a rock drawing the portrait, Jesus summons him and divines his mission. After reading the letter, Jesus responds with one of his own, writing, "Blessed are you, Abgar, in that you believed in me without having actually seen me." Jesus says that although he must fulfill his mission on earth, he will send one of the disciples to cure Abgar's suffering and to "also provide your city with a sufficient defence to keep all your enemies from taking it." After entrusting the letter to Ananias, says the official account, "The Savior then washed his face in water, wiped off the moisture that was left on the towel that was given to him, and in some divine and inexpressible manner had his own likeness impressed on it." Jesus gave Ananias the towel to present to Abgar as "consolation" for his disease.

This official account of the image, dating from the tenth century, notes, "there is another story about this [cloth] which is neither incredible nor short of reliable witnesses." In this second version, the image is impressed with Jesus' bloody sweat during his agony in the Garden of Gethsemane (Luke 22:44):

> They say that when Christ was about to go voluntarily to death he was seen to reveal his human weakness, feel anguish, and pray. According to the Evangelist, sweat dropped from him like drops of blood.

> Then they say he took this piece of cloth which we see now from one of the disciples and wiped off the drops of sweat on it. At once the still-visible impression of that divine face was produced.

The tale continues with Jesus giving the cloth to Thomas for safekeeping until after Jesus has ascended into heaven, at which time "the divine portrait of Christ's face" is to be taken by Thaddaeus to King Abgar. Subsequently, Abgar supposedly touched the magical cloth to the afflicted parts of his body and was cleansed of his leprosy (Wilson 1979, 272–90).

The noted historian Sir Steven Runciman denounces both versions of the story as apocryphal (while conceding that this does not necessarily debunk the tradition on which the tales are based). Runciman states, "It is easy to show that the story of Abgar and Jesus as we now have it is untrue, that the letters contained phrases copied from the gospels and are framed according to the dictates of later theology" (quoted in Sox 1978, 52).

Veronica's Veil

In a later version of this tale, the impressed cloth is called Veronica's Veil to distinguish it from the image of Edessa (later called the Mandylion). According to pious legend, Veronica, a woman from Jerusalem, was so moved by Jesus' struggle with the cross on the way to Golgotha that she wiped his face with her veil or kerchief, on which his portrait was imprinted in bloody sweat (see figures 4.2 and 4.3). In some versions, Veronica gives the veil to Jesus so that he might wipe his brow, and he miraculously imprints his face on it. (Except as noted, this discussion is from Wilson 1979, 106–21; *Encyclopaedia Britannica* 1960, s.v. "Veronica, Saint"; and Nickell 1998, 45–48.)

The Veronica tradition clearly derives from the Edessan one, which has been traced to an account (circa 325) by Bishop Eusebius. It mentions the Abgar–Jesus correspondence and a woman (not Veronica) with an "issue of blood" who is cured when she touches Jesus' garment (Mark 5:25–34; Matthew 9:20–22; Luke 8:43–48). But Eusebius omits the figured cloth from his Abgar–Jesus account, and all descriptions of such imprinted veils date from later times—the earliest cer-

(Above) Figure 4.2. Veronica offers her veil to Jesus to wipe his face (mid-nineteenth-century illustration by Julius Schnorr von Carolsfeld).
(Below) Figure 4.3. Veronica displays her veil—miraculously imprinted with Jesus' face (author's collection).

tain reference probably being the fourth-century *Doctrine of Addai.* In the official, tenth-century account of the image of Edessa, it was said to be "without coloring." Elsewhere it was described as being "due to sweat, not pigments" and "not consist[ing] of earthly colors."

It is not surprising that many of these figured cloths appeared. According to Thomas Humber (1978, 92), "Soon the popular demand for more copies representing the 'true likeness' of Christ was such that selected artists were allowed or encouraged to make duplications." Indeed, "there was, conveniently, another tradition supporting the copies: the Image could miraculously duplicate itself." These copies eventually came to be known as *veronicas*—the term being a corruption of the words *vera iconica* ("true images"; the two words are Latin, the second deriving from the Greek *eikon*). In what appears to be a further corruption, dating from the fifteenth century, the cloth is sometimes referred to as "the holy vernicle of Rome." These veronicas were "supposedly miraculous, but, in fact, painted" (Humber 1978, 85). Nevertheless, Veronica's Veil was among the venerated "great relics of the Crucifixion" (Barber 2004, 118). (See figure 4.4.)

Today, one such holy image—kept at a church in the village of Manoppello, Italy—has been known only since the mid-seventeenth century, when it appeared under curious circumstances. The "unknown pilgrim" who bestowed the rolled-up picture to a local astrologer was subsequently seen going into the church but—shades of the supernatural—was never seen leaving (Santuario 2005). The picture appears to be nothing more than an amateurishly rendered traditional likeness of Jesus. It is certainly a "positive" picture rather than a "negative" one, such as that caused by a facial imprint (see chapter 9).

As the Veronica legend evolved—Veronica the woman obviously being named after the image—it was included in the Holy Grail romances, including the original version of Robert de Boron's *L'Estoire dou Graal* (The History of the Grail), circa 1200. It is part of the story of Pontius Pilate following the events surrounding Jesus' death. The veronica's appearance in the Grail romances is significant because it "introduces another object with a physical link to the Crucifixion" (Barber 2004, 127)—even if it is a manufactured one.

Figure 4.4. This "veronica," featuring a copperplate engraving on linen, was a souvenir of the Vatican, circa late eighteenth century (author's collection).

As the Veronica tale became part of the mythologizing process related to the Crucifixion, it took its place in a series of "stations of the cross." According to the *Catholic Dictionary*, this is "a devotional practice that *reconstructs* the events in the life of our Lord from His trial to His entombment" (Stravinskas 2002, 710; emphasis added). Those stations are as follows:

> (1) Jesus is condemned; (2) Jesus carries His Cross; (3) Jesus falls the first time; (4) Jesus meets His mother; (5) Simon of Cyrene helps carry the Cross; (6) Veronica wipes Jesus' face; (7) Jesus falls a second time; (8) Jesus meets the women of Jerusalem; (9) Jesus falls the third time; (10) Jesus is stripped of His garments; (11) Jesus is nailed to the Cross; (12) Jesus dies on the Cross; (13) Jesus' Body is taken down from the Cross; (14) Jesus' Body is laid in the tomb. Some modern stations add a fifteenth for Jesus' resurrection.

The veronica images not only proliferated but also expanded in physical scope. Whereas the early Mandylion and veronica images were face-only portraits, a thirteenth-century author described a veronica depicting Jesus "from the chest upwards." Also, from as early as the twelfth century, the Mandylion is sometimes described as bearing "the glorious image of the Lord's face and the length of his whole body" and "the likeness and proportions of the body of the Lord." By the thirteenth century, we find this amplification in the story of Jesus giving his portrait to King Abgar: "For it is handed down from archives of ancient authority that the Lord prostrated himself full length on most white linen, and so by divine power the most beautiful likeness not only of the face, but also of the whole body of the Lord was impressed upon the cloth" (Wilson 1998, 108, 115, 158, 159). Although these full-length images were supposedly of the living Jesus, they set the stage for the appearance—in the mid-fourteenth century—of the Shroud of Turin, with its imprint of an apparently crucified Christ (see chapters 8 and 9).

In 1907, upon opening the silver reliquary in St. Peter's that supposedly held the Veil of Veronica, Monsignor Joseph Wilpert saw only "a square piece of light-colored material, somewhat faded through age, which bore two faint, irregular rust-brown stains, connected one to the other" (Wilson 1979, 107). This relic had supposedly been seized and lost in the 1527 sacking of Rome by the troops of Charles V. But if that is true, how do we account for the cloth found in the reliquary? Was it merely an artist's copy? Surely, if we can believe Wilpert's description—and "modern enquiries meet with almost no information from Vatican custodians" (Wilson 1979, 107)—this object was not an obvious artist's copy; possibly it was a replacement (Nickell 1998, 46).

In *Relics*, Joan Carroll Cruz (1984, 56) has this to say about the veil enshrined in St. Peter's:

> Veronica is said to have bequeathed the veil to Clement I, the third successor of St. Peter. During the three centuries of persecution the relic was kept in the depths of the catacombs, but was afterwards placed in the church constructed over the tomb of St. Peter. It is in this church, that developed into the Basilica of St. Peter, that the Holy Face has been kept from the earliest times. It is now preserved in the chapel constructed in one of the four enormous pillars that sustained the cupola of St. Peter's. Adorned by Bernini with balustrades and niches and surrounded by twisted columns from the ancient church, the pier is fronted by an enormous statue of Veronica that stands 16

feet tall. It seems one of the movements captured in stone. With her extended arm producing a sweep of the veil, Veronica seems to have been halted between the excitement of her discovery and her eagerness to exhibit the holy treasure of the Lord's likeness. A door arranged at the base of the statue gives access to two corridors, one leading to the Vatican grottoes where the relics of St. Peter repose, the other ascending to the interior niche where the Holy Icon is kept. The keys to the three locks affixed to the vault have been confided to the Canons of St. Peter's who are entrusted with the guardianship of the holy treasure. The veil is kept in a reliquary formed of a magnificent frame of crystal and silver gilt.

Lest anyone doubt the authenticity of Veronica's Veil, Cruz (1984, 56) states:

Early writers maintain that there cannot be the slightest doubt regarding the icon's genuineness. Father John van Bolland (1596–1665), whose name was adopted by the Bollandists, the Jesuit editor of the *Acta Sanctorum*, informs us that, "It is the unanimous opinion of all sacred historians and the firm belief of all true Christians that the Veronica seu Vultus Domini, now at Rome, is the identical and veritable cloth offered to the Redeemer on His way to Calvary." We are likewise told that St. Bridget, the visionary mystic, reproved anyone who doubted its authenticity. Confirmations were also made by various popes who permitted its mention in ancient ceremonials, bulls, and correspondence, and its celebration in festivals and processions.

So, despite its lack of provenance or any other evidence of genuineness (the pronouncements of a "visionary" aside), the question is settled—at least for the faithful, who need little to reassure them.

CHAPTER 5

The True Cross

As the central image of Christianity, the cross on which Jesus was crucified is among the most powerful of all symbols and relics (see figure 5.1). The story of the True Cross involves its alleged revelation to St. Helena, the recovery of the Holy Cross and the *Titulus* (title board), and the proliferation and dispensation of fragments and nails from the cross.

Visions of Constantine and Helena

The story of the purported discovery of the True Cross begins with Constantine the Great (274–337), who became sole emperor of the Roman Empire. Constantine was the out-of-wedlock son of Constantius Chlorus and Flavia Helena, who (according to Milan's St. Ambrose) was an innkeeper's daughter. During his rise to power, while in danger of defeat by the tyrannical Maxentius, Constantine supposedly experienced a miraculous vision of a flaming cross that appeared in the noonday sky, together with the words "In this sign conquer." The vision led to Constantine's conversion to Christianity, and with his soldiers' shields and banners emblazoned with Christ's monogram, he won Rome from the pagans (Thiede and d'Ancona 2002, 1–37; Cruz 1984, 38–41; *Encyclopaedia Britannica* 1960, s.v. "Constantine," "Helena, St."). Later, Constantine formally recognized Chris-

Figure 5.1. Jesus dies on a cross, which becomes the emblem of Christianity (mid-nineteenth-century illustration by Julius Schnorr von Carolsfeld).

tianity, protected its practitioners from persecution, and chose Byzantium as the new capital (see figure 5.2). He renamed it Constantinople after himself (city of Constantine). It appears that the epithet "Great" referred to neither his intellectual nor his moral strengths but to his empire building.

The fanciful story of Constantine's miraculous vision does not withstand scrutiny. The earliest account, written by a credible contemporary, makes no mention of such a celestial event, claiming—much less dramatically—that Constantine saw the sign of the cross in a dream. Only in a later account, *Life of Constantine* by Eusebius (circa 260–340), does the daytime-sky miracle appear, and even that is supplemented by a description of a dream the emperor had the fol-

Figure 5.2. The Byzantine cross (circa seventh century) was a legacy of Constantine the Great, who made Christianity the Roman Empire's official religion (author's collection).

lowing night. Although Eusebius professed to have heard the claim from the emperor's own lips, he wrote after Constantine's death, and since he omitted it from his earlier *Ecclesiastical History* (completed in 324 or early 325), the miraculous apparition was apparently unknown to him at that writing (*Encyclopaedia Britannica* 1960, s.v. "Constantine").

We should invoke here a skeptical axiom described by Robert Price (2003, 50), a noted biblical scholar and member of the Jesus Seminar:

> If we possess two versions of a story, one more and one less spectacular, if either is closer to the truth, it must be the latter. If the former, the more dramatic, were earlier, how can we explain the origin of the latter, the more conservative version? If the first story to be told were more spectacular, who would ever try to supplement it with a tamer one? But if the tamer tale were the first it is easier to see how later on someone might think a juicier version desirable.

Considering all the evidence, and applying this axiom, it appears that Eusebius was provided an embellished account of Constantine's vision. Indeed, "Eusebius is universally acknowledged to have been a partial, self-interested and often devious writer" (Thiede and d'Ancona 2002, 48).

However, it is another reputed vision—that of Constantine's mother, Queen Helena (later St. Helena)—that we are especially concerned with. According to pious legend, at the age of almost eighty, Helena was "advised by divinely-sent visions" to travel to Jerusalem, where she discovered, it was claimed, the True Cross on which Jesus had been crucified (Rufinus ca. 402). However, scrutiny of the legend is, once again, instructive and casts doubt on the tale.

First of all, even major defenders of the authenticity of the cross concede, "At this distance it is impossible to know exactly why the Empress Helena chose this moment in her life to embark upon her odyssey to the Near East" (Thiede and d'Ancona 2002, 38). Is it true that Constantine "dispatched" her there "to recover the True Cross and the relics of the Passion," as reported by Cruz (1984, 38)? Or was it, as some historians have speculated, "to do penance and to atone for her sins in the last years of her life"? Possibly it was even "the mystical allure of the holy places" (Thiede and d'Ancona 2002, 39).

In any event, in 326 Helena went to Jerusalem, where she allegedly discovered the place where the cross was concealed, supposedly with the help of divine inspiration. Unfortunately, but perhaps not surprisingly, we learn that "slightly different versions of the findings have come down to us" (Cruz 1984, 38). Indeed, some claimed that Helena actually discovered the site of the True Cross not by signs or dreams, as often alleged, but with "the guidance of a Jew called Judas" (Thiede and d'Ancona 2002, 22).

The legend first appears in an account *De Obitu Theodosii* (the funeral oration of Emperor Theodosius the Great) by Ambrose, Bishop of Milan, written in 395 but apparently based on an earlier source. However, these accounts were written in the West long after Helena's death. Chroniclers in Jerusalem much closer to the event were unaware of Helena's alleged discovery of the cross (*Encyclopaedia Britannica* 1960, s.v. "Helena, St."). A quite literary version of Helena's legendary discovery of the *Vera Crux*—the True Cross—was written by a scholarly monk named Rufinus in about 402. He states:

Helena, the mother of Constantine, a woman of outstanding faith and deep piety, and also of exceptional munificence, whose offspring indeed one would expect to be such a man as Constantine, was advised by divinely-sent visions to go to Jerusalem. There she was to make an enquiry among the inhabitants to find out the place where the sacred body of Christ had hung on the Cross. The spot was difficult to find, because the persecutors of old had set a statue of Venus over it, so that if any Christian wanted to worship Christ in that place, he seemed to be worshipping Venus. For this reason, the place was not much frequented and had all but been forgotten.

Rufinus refers to a pagan temple, Aelia Capitolina, which the Emperor Hadrian had built on the site of the Holy Sepulchre.

But when, as we related above, the pious lady hastened to the spot pointed out to her by a heavenly sign, she tore down all that was profane and polluted there. Deep beneath the rubble she found three crosses lying in disorder. But the joy of finding this treasure was marred by difficulty of distinguishing to whom each cross belonged. The board was there, it is true, on which Pilate had placed an inscription written in Greek, Latin and Hebrew characters. But not even this provided sufficient evidence to identify the Lord's Cross. In such an ambiguous case uncertainty requires divine proof. It happened that in that same city, a certain prominent lady of that place lay mortally ill with a serious disease. Macarius was at that time bishop of the Church there. When he saw the doubts of the queen and all present, he said: "Bring all three crosses which have been found and God will now reveal to us which is the cross which bore Christ."

After a prayer by Bishop Macarius, the "wood of salvation" was brought near the woman, and she was miraculously healed.

When the queen saw that her wish had been answered by such a clear sign, she built a marvellous church of royal magnificence over the place where she had discovered the Cross. The nails, too, which had attached the Lord's body to the Cross, she sent to her son. From some of these he had a horse's bridle made, for use in battle, while he used the others to add strength to a helmet, equally with a view to using it in battle. Part of the redeeming wood she sent to her son, but she also left part of it there preserved in silver chests. This part is commemorated by regular veneration to this very day. (quoted in Thiede and d'Ancona 2002, 20–22)

A moment's reflection shows how implausible this tale is, beginning with the notion that not only Jesus' cross but also the crosses of the "two thieves crucified with him" (Matthew 27:38) were interred with his body in the tomb. Neither the Gospels nor any other prior source ever suggested such a thing. Added to that absurdity are the supposed divine revelation of the crosses' location and the identification of Christ's cross by means of a miraculous cure. We should recognize the entire tale for the fantasy it is.

The Holy Cross

The legend of the Holy Cross's imagined pre-Christian history is no less a fabrication. That tale is told in a compendium of saints' lives and miraculous events called *The Golden Legend*, written by Jacobus de Voragine in the thirteenth century. Jacobus claimed that an angel had given one of Adam's sons, Seth, a branch of the tree from the Garden of Eden that had borne the forbidden fruit (Genesis 3:1–24) and informed him "that when that branch bore fruit, his father would be made whole." Seth, the legend continues, planted the branch at Adam's grave, where it grew into a tree that was still standing in the time of Solomon. The king used it to construct a bridge over a pond, but the Queen of Sheba "saw in spirit that the Savior of the world would one day hang upon this very same wood." Indeed, *The Golden Legend* reports, the wood later "floated up to the surface of the pond, and the Jews, seeing it, used it in making the Lord's cross." In repeating this tale, Thiede and d'Ancona (2002, 9) acknowledge—with understatement—that "Jacobus was a devotional writer and a fabulist rather than a historian."

The cross's history after its alleged rediscovery by Helena is less fantastic. A portion was supposedly given to Constantine, and another was taken to Rome. The main portion was kept in the custody of successive bishops of Jerusalem, being exhibited only at the most significant religious ceremonies. However, in 614—when the Persians, under King Khosroes II, invaded Palestine and reportedly killed sixty thousand defenders—the cross was carried off, along with some thirty-five thousand slaves. But its captivity was short-lived; in 627, Byzantine emperor Heraclius I defeated the Persian forces at Nineveh in Mesopotamia and subsequently returned triumphantly to Jerusalem bearing the Holy Cross (Thiede and d'Ancona 2002, 6–7; Cruz 1984, 40).

For more than half a millennium, the *Vera Crux* continued to repose in Jerusalem. Then in 1187 it was again lost—this time forever. The crusading Franks had occupied Jerusalem for eighty-eight years (see figure 5.3) when the Egyptian sultan Saladin (1138–1193) sought to reconquer the city. The Frankish army met the sultan's army at Hattin on the plain of Galilee, with the bishop of Acre holding aloft the True Cross. When the battle ended, Saladin was victorious, the bishop of Acre was dead, and, according to Thiede and d'Ancona (2002, 8):

> Once again, the Christian world had lost its most precious relic. Richard the Lionheart tried later to recover it in the 1190s, as did the Queen of Georgia who offered a 200,000 dinars ransom. But the Cross was not to be returned at any cost. Myths swirled around its eventual fate; it was said that the Templars had buried it somewhere, perhaps in the Holy Land, perhaps in France. Three centuries later the Christians of Constantinople claimed to have the wood in their possession, but to no avail. As far as Christendom was concerned, the *Vera Crux* had been lost for ever on the field of Hattin.

No useful description of the cross, even the one allegedly discovered by Helena, remains. Based on an "ancient" but "dubious" tradition, the upright was almost 189 inches long and extended above the crossbeam, which was between 90½ and 102½ inches long (Cruz 1984, 41). The lack of any contemporary description of the alleged True Cross extends to the Gospels. The evangelists mention only "the cross" (Matthew 27:40) and "the cross of Jesus" (John 19:25), without further characterization.

The idea that Jesus carried a cross to Golgotha (see figure 5.4) is probably incorrect. The Romans used a vertical post called a *stipes* that was permanently set in the ground at the place of execution; the victim was forced to carry the *patibulum,* or crossbeam, to the site. With his arms outstretched, he was nailed to the beam, which was then hoisted up and secured to the stipes; finally, his feet were nailed

Figure 5.3. When the crusaders captured Jerusalem in 1099, they also captured the True Cross. It was then lost forever when the city was recaptured by Saladin in 1187 (from *Proctor's History of the Crusades*).

(Ward 1987, 257, 259; Craveri 1967, 413). An upright with a transverse beam is therefore a reasonable portrayal in Christian art, although the *suppedaneum,* the foot support shown in depictions of the Crucifixion, did not exist (Craveri 1967, 413). The earliest Christian art showed Jesus' feel nailed separately; the crossed-feet, "three-nail-type" of contrivance was a later innovation (Nickell 1998, 64–65).

Figure 5.4. View of Golgotha, reportedly the site of Jesus' Crucifixion, is depicted in an old wood engraving (from Bennett 1882).

The sole archaeological example of an apparent first-century crucifixion victim shows a quite different method of nailing the feet. The remains of one Yehohanan, discovered near Jerusalem in 1968, include a heel bone with a nail penetrating it from the side. This indicates that "to hang him on the cross," his executioners "viciously bent his legs, forcing him into a sort of sidesaddle position and then driving the nail in from the side straight through the heel bones" (Wilson 1979, 50). Alternatively, his feet may have been "nailed to the cross separately, to the left and right of the vertical beam" (Thiede and d'Ancona 2002, 66–67). A bit of wood between the heel bone and the nail head indicated that a small board had been placed over the foot before nailing—either as a sort of clamp to keep the foot from tearing off the nail or, believes Wilson (1979, 49–51), as a plaque or *titulus* describing his offense. As discussed later, Jesus' own titulus was placed quite differently.

Interestingly, a church in Rome purports to have significant relics of the Crucifixion, including the *Titulus Crucis* (discussed in the next section) and the transverse beam from the cross of the penitent thief (the so-called good thief; see Luke 23:39–43). Pious tradition has given his name as Dismas. In *The Quest for the True Cross*, Thiede and d'Ancona (2002, 68) discuss this alleged Crucifixion relic:

> This piece of wood has been part of the church's collection since 1570, when it was discovered in the altar steps of the chapel dedicated to Helena. Although there is enough wood left for a dendrochronological analysis this has not yet been attempted. In theory, it is no less likely that a piece of wood of this size could have survived as long as tiny fragments—not least if it had been protected by the climate of Jerusalem for three centuries in an old cistern underneath Hadrian's temple. But even if we accept, for the sake of the argument and with no reason in our written sources to do so, that crosses or parts of crosses other than that of Jesus were preserved and sent abroad, there is still no way to find out whether it belonged to Dismas, to the other thief or even to any other crucified man among the hundreds put to death by the Romans in those years on a hill like Golgotha. Some observers have noticed that there are no nail marks in the Dismas bar and that this conforms to the iconography of many early paintings where the two thieves were tied to the cross (and may have survived longer than Jesus for that reason: see John 19:31–33). But the ends of that beam, which today measures 1.78 metres in length, are clearly and cleanly cut off, perilously close to the points where nails would have been made for a man of average size. Accident or design? It is surely impossible to say. Confident study of this relic must await dendrochronological analysis and a biological survey of the remains of flora found in the crevices of the wood.

Note that this plank has no connection whatsoever with Jerusalem or with Helena's alleged discovery. Its excavation at a site in Rome dedicated to Helena does not justify the assumption that it is the ancient artifact it is now supposed to be. One wonders: Was this the kind of evidence Helena herself relied on when she supposedly discovered the three crosses, including the *Vera Crux?*

The Titulus

A *titulus*—a placard bearing the accusation against a condemned man—is described in the Gospel narratives of Jesus' Crucifixion:

"And Pilate wrote a title" that was placed on Jesus' cross; it read

"'Jesus of Nazareth the King of the Jews' . . . written in Hebrew, and Greek, and Latin" (John 19:19–20).

"Set up over his head his accusation written," which read,
"'This is Jesus the King of the Jews'" (Matthew 27:37).

"And the superscription of his accusation was written over, 'The
King of the Jews'" (Mark 15:26).

"And a superscription also was written over him in letters of
Greek, and Latin, and Hebrew, 'This is the King of the Jews'"
(Luke 23:38).

Allegedly discovered by Helena with the three crosses in the
Holy Sepulchre was the *Titulus Crucis,* the inscribed headboard of
the Holy Cross. As mentioned in the previous section, the monk
Rufinus said of it: "The board was there, it is true, on which Pilate
had placed an inscription written in Greek, Latin and Hebrew characters." (However, it had apparently become dislodged so that Jesus'
cross had to be distinguished from the two others by a miracle.) Helena supposedly divided the Titulus into three parts: one for her, one
for Rome, and one, the largest portion, to remain in Jerusalem. In
about 383, a pilgrim named Egeria wrote that the bishop of Jerusalem kept the wood of the True Cross and the Titulus in a small box.
This suggests that by that time—less than six decades after Helena's
discovery—only a small portion of the two relics remained.

Today, what many believe is one of those fragments of the *Titulus Crucis* (see figure 5.5) is enshrined in the Church of Santa Croce
in Gerusalemme, Rome. It is kept in the church's Chapel of Relics
along with two reputed thorns from the mock crown placed on Jesus' head at the Crucifixion, a finger bone of doubting Thomas, and
the transverse bar of the cross of the penitent thief. What became of
the other two pieces of the Titulus is unknown, and to believers, the
substantive portion at Santa Croce is now simply thought of as the
Titulus. In the middle of the twelfth century, it was placed in a new
box distinguished by the seal of the titular cardinal, Gerardo Cac-

Figure 5.5. A portion of the *Titulus Crucis*—the alleged placard from Jesus' cross—is pictured on the cover of this book that argues for its authenticity as a piece of the True Cross (author's collection).

cianemici, who served as Pope Lucius II (1144–1145). Thus the box should date to 1144 or earlier, which was "about half a century before the great explosion in fake relics which followed the Crusaders' conquest of Byzantium, when such artifacts . . . became the increasingly devalued currency of religious and political ambition" (Thiede and d'Ancona 2002, 91).

Be that as it may, the relic was essentially a "secret treasure" until it was reportedly rediscovered three and a half centuries later. It came to light when a mosaic was being restored in 1492. The removal of some damaged stucco revealed a brick with the inscription, "TITVLVS CRVCIS." Behind this was a niche containing the box with the Titulus. Cruz (1984, 43) believes that the Titulus was hidden by clergymen in about 455 when "confronted by Visigoth attacks."

Arguing for the authenticity of the artifact, according to the authors of *The Quest for the True Cross* (Thiede and d'Ancona 2002, 93–100), are several factors, including the following: the wood is a Near Eastern variety, having originally been painted white (like Roman placards); the carved lettering, with traces of dark coloring, consists of three partial lines in Hebrew (or Aramaic), Greek, and Latin; and the writing style is consistent with first-century letter forms (Thiede is a papyrologist). Thiede and d'Ancona (2002, 94) also make much of the sequence of the three languages, which differs from that in either Luke or John (see earlier). They insist, "It goes without saying that a forger, working for Helena or for the Christian community of Jerusalem, would have followed the order of languages suggested in one of these two Gospels." But that kind of argument involves what one of my mentors, the late forgery expert Charles Hamilton, called "trying to psychoanalyze the dead." Forgers—particularly of another era—may do something cleverer or dumber or simply different from what we would expect.

With a sensational object such as the Titulus, however, the maxim that extraordinary claims require extraordinary evidence applies. This is especially true when there is a nonexistent, doubtful, or suspicious provenance. Specific anachronisms or other problematic elements may warrant a judgment that the object is at least questionable; further investigation may lead to an expert opinion that it is a fake. With the Titulus, several factors raise questions and, taken together, suggest that it is a probable forgery (Nickell 2004b). First, although the Hebrew or Aramaic letters are correctly written from right to left, so, incorrectly, are the Greek and Latin lines. Thiede and d'Ancona (2002, 95) see this mistake as "powerful evidence" against forgery, since a falsifier "would simply not have risked something so abnormal if his purpose was to establish the supposed authenticity of his work." They suggest that the scribe simply made a mistake or might have been caricaturing the Jewish manner of writing, yet they concede, "there is no contemporary or near-contemporary evidence for a whole text executed in this way." In contrast, as soon as I saw this astonishing error, I thought it a prima facie indication of spuriousness, based on my research on the history of writing (Nickell 1990).

Another paleographic error is found in the Greek line. Although it is written in mirror-image fashion from right to left, one letter—Z—is not reversed. This underscores the problematic nature of the writing and suggests that the writer may have been unfamiliar with the ancient languages. In addition, a number of spelling errors cast doubt on the inscription if we do not accept the rationalizations of Thiede and d'Ancona (2002, 96–100). Another suspicious element is the fact that the letters were actually incised into the wood and then painted. The carving seems to be a gratuitous enhancement, a sort of icing on the cake intended to make the Titulus seem more appropriately elegant and thus suitable for Jesus' status. Yet the treatment of Jesus described in the Gospels belies any such sense of exalted status. On the contrary, one would expect a hastily prepared placard intended to be used quickly and then discarded. The time-consuming process of gouging out the letters suggests the work of a careful (yet not especially competent) forger.

As it happens, since *The Quest for the True Cross* was published, the Titulus has been radiocarbon dated. An area from the back of the slab of walnut wood (species *Juglans regia*) that was "perfectly preserved" was sampled "in and around a knot in the wood" (Bella and Azzi 2002, 685). The samples were specially cleaned to remove contaminants and then subjected to the carbon-dating process. To verify the accuracy of the system, the scientists also dated control samples of varying ages, including a twelfth-century wood sample, part of a fourteenth-century plank, and wood from Roman ships of the first century. The results from the control samples indicated accurate functioning of the analytical system. The radiocarbon dating of the Titulus yielded a calendar age of A.D. 980 to 1146 (Bella and Azzi 2002). This date, of course, eliminates any possibility that the artifact is an authentic first-century relic of Christ's Crucifixion. It is, instead, fully consistent with the period (1144–1145) when the artifact was apparently acquired.

Fragments and Nails

One portion of the True Cross was reportedly retained in a silver reliquary in a basilica erected over the Holy Sepulchre where the crosses were discovered by Helena. Apparently, this was the piece lost in 1187. Another piece was said to have been given to Constantine, who enclosed it in a statue of himself as a talisman of protection for Constantinople. And another portion was taken to Rome by Helena, who erected the Santa Croce in Gerusalemme. Today, three pieces of the True Cross, each about six inches long, are kept in a cruciform reliquary there (Cruz 1984, 39).

Alleged fragments of the True Cross and Roman nails from the Crucifixion have proliferated. In the mid-fourth century, St. Cyril of Jerusalem (circa 315–386) wrote in his lectures, the *Catecheses*, that "already the whole world is filled with fragments of the wood of the Cross." Cyril added, "The holy wood of the Cross gives witness: It is here to be seen in this very day, and through those who take [pieces] from it in faith, it has from here already filled almost all the world" (quoted in Thiede and d'Ancona 2002, 53). According to *The Quest for the True Cross:*

> There is corroboration for Cyril's claim that fragments of the Cross were spreading "around the world." As early as 359, a "martyrium" near Tixter in Mauretania boasted the deposit of a piece: a *"memoria sa[n]cta de lingo crucis."* According to Gregory of Nyssa, St. Macrina, who died in 379, used to wear a relic of the Cross in his locket. Towards the end of the fourth century, John Chrysostom noted that everyone was "fighting over" fragments of the wood. By the beginning of the fifth, there is evidence of such relics reaching Gaul, Africa, Asia Minor, Syria, Italy and elsewhere. (Thiede and d'Ancona 2002, 54)

From the fifth century on, a "cult of the cross" developed and "gave rise to the building of many churches and oratories as a worthy treasury of their relics" (Cruz 1984, 40). These included churches erected in the True Cross's name, such as Santa Croce at Ravenna, Italy, built before 450. In the 460s, Pope Hilarius constructed an oratory (a small chapel) for a relic of the cross in the Lateran. Similarly, Pope Symmiachus (498–514) placed a fragment in a golden cross-shaped reliquary in a specially built oratory at St. Peter's.

Fragments of the True Cross became so prolific, said Protestant John Calvin (1543, 61), that there were enough to "form a whole ship's cargo" (see figure 1.2). In a letter, St. Paulinus of Nola (353–431) explained that, regardless of how many pieces were taken from the cross, it never diminished in size—a "fact" that has been compared to the miracle of the multiplying loaves and fishes (Cruz 1984, 39). (In the nineteenth century, a Frenchman measured as many pieces of the cross as he could find and reported that they totaled only 4 million cubic millimeters; the cross on which Jesus was crucified, he argued, probably contained as many as 178 million cubic millimeters [Meyer 1971, 73].)

Some disdained the coveting of wooden relics. St. Jerome (circa 342–420) took pains to say, "By the cross I mean not the wood, but the Passion. That cross is in Britain, in India, in the whole world. . . . Happy is he who carries in his own heart the cross, the resurrection, the place of the Nativity of Christ and of his Ascension." And Milan's St. Ambrose (circa 339–397) cautioned against venerating the wood itself, "for that is the error of pagans and the folly of the unrighteous" (quoted in Thiede and d'Ancona 2002, 55).

The True Cross's seventh-century recovery from the Persians and its return to Jerusalem by Byzantine emperor Heraclius I is still commemorated annually in Paris. The September 14 feast, the Triumph of the Cross, was specially observed in 1241 when King Louis removed his regal robes and walked barefoot in a procession carrying a fragment of the *Sacré Croix* (Cruz 1984, 40). Reputedly, in seventh-century Jerusalem, pilgrim tokens (like the one shown in figure 5.6) were produced, possibly as a means of multiplying the sought-after relic. The tokens, made of clay allegedly mixed with a bit of ash from a burned piece of the True Cross, were crudely embossed with figures beneath a large image of the cross.

Among the relics of the Passion, the True Cross is the central icon, but there are also nails to provide a touch of gruesome reality to the story of Christ's Crucifixion. The Gospels provided little detail; however, self-proclaimed visionaries could elaborate, as did Anne Catherine Emmerich (1774–1824), whose bloodthirsty imaginings were a major source for Mel Gibson's controversial 2004 movie *The Passion of the Christ*. She wrote, for instance, about the nailing of Jesus to the cross (Emmerich 1904, 172):

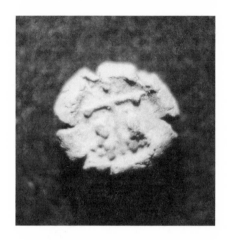

Figure 5.6. Embossed pilgrims' tokens of the True Cross were reputedly made in the seventh century by mixing clay with some ash from a burned piece of the cross (author's collection).

The executioners did not allow him to rest long, but bade him rise and place himself on the cross that they might nail him to it. Then, seizing his right arm, they dragged it to the hole prepared for the nail, and having tied it tightly down with a cord, one of them knelt upon his sacred chest, a second held his hand flat, and a third taking a long thick nail, pressed it on the open palm of that adorable hand, which had ever been open to bestow blessings and favors on the ungrateful, and with a great iron hammer drove it through the flesh, and far into the wood of the cross. Our Lord uttered one deep but suppressed groan, and his blood gushed forth and sprinkled the arms of the archers. I counted the blows of the hammer, but my extreme grief made me forget their number. The nails were very large, the heads about the size of a crown piece, and the thickness that of a man's thumb, while the points came through at the back of the cross. . . . This dreadful process caused our Lord indescribable agony, his breast heaved, and his legs were quite contracted.

Emmerich continues in this dubiously inspired fashion.

What we know of actual crucifixion nails comes from the previously mentioned remains of Yehohanan, uncovered in 1968. A single nail is 12 centimeters long (about 4¾ inches) and 0.9 centimeter wide on each of its four sides—Roman nails being square rather than round. (Interestingly, the alleged stigmatic Therese Neumann first exhibited round "nail wounds" in her hands, but these shifted to squarish ones over time, presumably as she learned the true shape of Roman nails [Nickell 2001, 278].) The various "true nails" that appeared over time apparently resembled real Roman nails, but these have always been available and could easily be passed off as nails from the Crucifixion—with a suitable tale to accompany them.

According to St. Ambrose, after Helena's supposed discovery of the Holy Sepulchre, she sent two nails to Constantine, leaving one or two unaccounted for (depending on whether one or two were used to nail the feet, as discussed previously). Legends say that Constantine attached one to his helmet, and the other was supposedly attached to his horse's bridle; however, St. Gregory of Tours (538–594)—a collector of pious legends—claimed that the second nail was fashioned as a bit for the horse. Supposedly this was intended to fulfill the Old Testament prophecy of Zechariah, which Cruz (1984, 42) gives as follows: "In that day that which is upon the bridle of the horse shall be holy to the Lord." However, other translations state "bit" instead of "bridle," and the King James version reads, "In that day shall there be upon the bells of the horses, HOLINESS UNTO THE LORD" (Zechariah 14:20).

Helena is said to have sent one nail (together with a segment of the True Cross and the previously discussed piece of the Titulus) to Rome's Church of Santa Croce in Gerusalemme. It still reposes there in its reliquary, but its head has been replaced, raising various questions (Cruz 1984, 42; Thiede and d'Ancona 2002, 66–67). And if no one is counting, we might consider another pious legend that relates how Helena threw one of the holy nails into the Gulf of Venice to quell a storm (Nickell 1998, 52). But count we must. Other nails have appeared, including one at the Notre Dame Cathedral in Paris; another at the cathedral in Trier, Germany; and still another in Florence. In fact, some thirty nails have been claimed by churches across Europe. As with pieces of the True Cross, means were found to multiply them. For example, filings from "true nails" were included with the metal nails forged to resemble them, and imitation nails were made that were touched to a supposed original. St. Charles Borromeo reportedly produced many such replica nails at Milan and distributed them as mementos. "We can only suppose," states Cruz (1984, 42), "that these nails, originally identified as imitations that touched the true nails, later lost their true identity with the passage of time until both clergy and faithful, in good faith, accepted them as authentic."

Perhaps. But relics of the Crucifixion were eagerly sought by noblemen and churches alike in order to enhance their influence, and there were always those willing to supply them—even if by unholy means.

CHAPTER 6

Other Crucifixion Relics

In addition to the True Cross and related items, there are other reputed relics of the Crucifixion. These include relics of the trial and scourging, the crown of thorns, the holy garments, and the so-called lance of Longinus.

Relics of the Trial and Scourging

In Rome, near the Lateran Basilica, is a sanctuary that originally served as the chapel of the papal palace (until the schism in the church from 1309 to 1378, when the papacy was relocated in Avignon, France). Here is a twenty-eight-step marble staircase known as the *Scala Sancta* (Holy Staircase), supposedly from Pontius Pilate's palace. According to tradition, the steps were those Jesus climbed during the evening of his Passion, making his way to Pilate's Jerusalem courtroom. Like the True Cross, the Titulus, the nails, and other relics of the Passion, the Holy Staircase was allegedly transported from Jerusalem to Rome by Queen Helena, the greatest relic acquirer of legend.

Joan Carroll Cruz, in her book *Relics* (1984, 32), tells how the stairs attract the faithful:

> At all times of the day pilgrims are seen ascending the steps on their knees and reverently kissing the glass panes marking the places

touched by the Savior's bleeding feet. Many popes have likewise climbed these stairs, including Gelasius I, Gregory the Great, Sergius I, Stephen III, Leo IV, Gregory VII and St. Leo III, who often went there to meditate on the Sacred Passion. On the eve of the invasion of Rome by the troops of Victor Emmanuel, Pope Pius IX climbed the stairs on his knees in spite of his 78 years.

To aid in the descent, two flights of steps, one on either side of the Holy Stairs, have been constructed so that the pilgrim may walk away without disturbing those still ascending.

As poignant as such devotions are, the question is, are the stairs really from Pilate's palace? Actually, the *Scala Sancta* is associated with Helena only by a legend that is as tenuous as it is late. It "can hardly claim to be authentic," insist Thiede and d'Ancona (2002, 65). They observe that the staircase was actually "installed at an unknown date" and explain:

> It is not the kind of relic uniquely related to Jesus in which Helena would have been interested. In any case the Jerusalem Praetorium of the Roman governor was not a permanent building: the administrative seat was in Caesarea and Pilate, his predecessors and successors only went to Jerusalem on special occasions, staying at one of the Herodian residences. This means it is much less likely that Macarius [bishop of Jerusalem] and his team of excavators would have been certain where to look for the "authentic" steps—if they ever existed.

They continue: "In fact, modern archaeological research has shown that the provisional Praetorium of Pilate was not where the *Via Dolorosa* [the route Jesus took to Golgotha] followed by contemporary pilgrims supposes it to be." Indeed, at the supposed site, "there are no traces of ancient stairs, removed or otherwise" (Thiede and d'Ancona 2002, 65–66).

Marcello Craveri (1967, 411) agrees that the *Via Dolorosa* (Way of Sorrow) or *Via Crucis* (Way of the Cross) is an erroneous route. He states that pilgrims seeking to honor Jesus' martyrdom "followed a route that in fact he had never taken." Moreover, Craveri states emphatically, "There is no validity to the location of the so-called stations of the cross: the places where he first stumbled, where he encountered his mother, where he stumbled again, etc." He concludes, "Of the fourteen stations, only two mark incidents reported in the Gospels: the meetings with Simon the Cyrenian and with the group of pious women."

Mark Twain, in *The Innocents Abroad* (1869, 430), reported on his own walking of the "Sorrowful Way, or the Way of Grief." He could scarcely contain his sarcasm as he reported seeing "the very window from which Pilate's wife warned her husband to have nothing to do with the persecution of the Just Man," adding, "this window is in an excellent state of preservation, considering its great age." A bit later, he reported:

> At the next corner we saw a deep indentation in the hard stone masonry of the corner of the house, but might have gone heedlessly by it but that the guide said it was made by the elbow of the Saviour, who stumbled here and fell. Presently we came to just such another indentation in a stone wall. The guide said the Saviour fell here, also, and made this depression with his elbow. (Twain 1869, 431)

Even though so many sites related to Jesus' Crucifixion were actually unknown, the scourging post, the pillar at which Jesus was flogged (Mark 15:15), was somehow identified—or so it is said. Preserved in Rome, the post, which is only about thirty-two inches tall, is of a variegated, blue-and-white oriental chalcedony. Enclosed in a tapered glass case and displayed in an ornate stand, it reposes behind an iron grille in a small chapel of the Church of St. Praxedes (Craveri 1967, 403; Cruz 1984, 33–34).

The little pillar has no documented history before 1223, however, when Cardinal John Colonna brought it to Rome from Constantinople. Despite this paucity of evidence, Cruz (1984, 33) finds it similar to a stone column in a chapel in Jerusalem, supposedly built over Pilate's palace courtyard. Cruz also cites the dubious visions of the mystic Anne Catherine Emmerich (1904, 134), who writes, "This pillar, placed in the center of the court, stood alone, and did not serve to sustain any part of the building; it was not very high, for a tall man could touch the summit by stretching out his arm; there was a large iron ring at the top, and both rings and hooks a little lower down." Clearly, Emmerich was not describing the post in Rome, which is far

Figure 6.1. Collection of relics from Constantinople—including an alleged segment of the post at which Jesus was scourged—is displayed at St. Mark's Basilica in Venice (photo by author).

shorter and lacks the iron rings and hooks. Nevertheless, she portrays "the Jewish mob" looking on as the scourging is carried out. The actual whipping was not done with a Roman *flagrum*, which left wounds supposedly like those pictured on the Shroud of Turin (see chapter 9) and shown in medieval paintings (Nickell 1998, 59–60). Instead, Emmerich "saw" whips or flexible rods, then "a different kind of rod—a species of thorny stick, covered with knots and splinters." Inflicted on Jesus, "the blows from these sticks tore his flesh to pieces; his blood spouted out so as to stain their arms, and he groaned, prayed, and shuddered" (Emmerich 1904, 135).

If the little pillar in Rome is not the true scourging post, then there is another in Venice at St. Mark's Basilica, which I visited in 2004. It is reportedly only a lower segment of the column and is on display along with other relics from Constantinople (see figure 6.1). It too lacks any meaningful proof of authenticity.

Mark Twain encountered yet another alleged segment of the pillar, which the priests tried to show to him and his companion through a screen. "But we could not see it because it was dark inside the screen. However, a baton is kept here, which the pilgrim thrusts through a hole in the screen, and then he no longer doubts that the true Pillar of Flagellation is in there. He can not have any excuse to doubt it, for he can feel it with the stick. He can feel it as distinctly as he could feel any thing" (Twain 1869, 420).

The Crown of Thorns

In *The Innocents Abroad*, Twain (1869, 425) also tells of visiting Jerusalem's Chapel of the Mocking: "Under the altar was a fragment of a marble column; this was the seat Christ sat on when he was reviled, and mockingly made King, crowned with a crown of thorns and sceptered with a reed. It was here that they blindfolded him and struck him, and said in derision, 'Prophesy who it is that smote thee.'" Here Twain adds with his dry wit: "The tradition that this is the identical spot of the mocking is a very ancient one. The guide said that Saewulf was the first to mention it. I do not know Saewulf, but still, I cannot well refuse to receive his evidence—none of us can."

Three of the evangelists mention the crown of thorns. For example, according to Mark (15:15–20):

> And so Pilate, willing to content the people, released Barabbas unto them, and delivered Jesus, when he had scourged him, to be crucified.
> And the soldiers led him away into the hall, called Praetorium; and they called together the whole band. And they clothed him with purple and plaited a crown of thorns, and put it about his head. And began to salute him, "Hail, King of the Jews!" And they smote him on the head with a reed, and did spit upon him, and bowing their knees worshipped him. And when they had mocked him, they took off the purple from him, and put his own clothes on him, and led him out to crucify him.

Mark says nothing further about the crown. Matthew (27:29) only repeats Mark, as does John (19:2); Luke does not mention the crown, writing only that "Herod with his men of war set him at nought, and

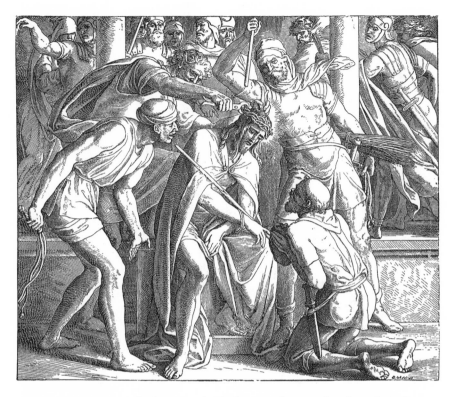

Figure 6.2. "Jesus with the Crown of Thorns" depicts the plaited circlet that is usually portrayed in art and was claimed to exist as early as the fourth century (mid-nineteenth-century illustration by Julius Schnorr von Carolsfeld).

mocked *him*, and arrayed him in a gorgeous robe, and sent him again to Pilate" (Luke 23:11). Lacking any description or guidelines, visionaries and artists—as well as manufacturers of fake relics—have imagined two basic styles: either a circlet, like a wreath that went around the head, or a bonnet-style crown that covered the top of the head. Both forms are seen in Christian art. Shroud of Turin advocates believe that they see the effect of the latter on that alleged relic's image (see chapter 9).

The crown of thorns was first acknowledged as existing in the fourth century (see figure 6.2). St. Paulinus of Nola noted, "The thorns with which Our Saviour was crowned was held in honor together with the Holy Cross and the pillar of the scourging" (quoted in Cruz 1984, 34). The credulous were told that the crown was discovered by none other than Helena when she opened the Holy Sepulchre. Twain (1869, 424) described the cavernous Chapel of St. Helena, featuring a marble chair on which the empress sat while superintending the workmen as they excavated the grotto. Cruz states (1984, 35), "It is certain that what was purported to be the Crown of Our Lord was venerated at Jerusalem for several hundred years."

In about 570, Cassiodorus observed that at Jerusalem "we may behold the thorny crown, which was set upon the head of the Redeemer." And St. Gregory of Tours (538–594) claimed that the crown's thorns still appeared green, its freshness being "miraculously renewed each day" (quoted in Cruz 1984, 35).

The crown was taken in about 1063 to Constantinople, where the emperor's palace had almost a complete set of relics of the Passion. In addition to a cross, nails, and lance, there was a sponge and hyssop reed, together with burial linens and a pair of Jesus' sandals (Nickell 1998, 52). States one source (Gies and Gies 1990, 295): "The Crown of Thorns, pawned by the new Latin emperor to the Venetians, was eventually purchased by St. Louis, who built the Sainte-Chapelle [1243–1248] to receive it, apparently regarding it as superior in authenticity to the two other Crowns of Thorns that Paris already possessed."

This crown was lodged in the Bibliothèque Nationale during the French Revolution, restored to the Sainte Chapelle in 1806, and eventually transferred to Notre Dame Cathedral, where it is kept in an elaborate reliquary. Botanical studies have identified the plant from which the crown was fashioned as Christ's-thorn (*Paliurus spina-christi*), a type of bush that is abundant around Jerusalem.

Twain (1869, 125, 194) delighted in pointing out that whereas one fragment of the crown of thorns was at St. Peter's in Rome and another at Milan Cathedral, "they have a whole one at Notre Dame." But apologists have another view, noting that the Notre Dame crown is a circlet, completely devoid of thorns. It has been suggested that it originally had the helmet form, as "seen" by the supposed visionary St.

Bridget (1303–1373) and others. Cruz (1984, 34) states, "It is believed that the upper part and all the thorns were distributed as relics."

Fragments alleged to be from the crown of thorns are kept in the Parochial Church of Weverlghem in Belgium and at churches in Trier, Germany, and Pisa, Italy. The latter is an eight-centimeter branch with three of its four thorns remaining. It was acquired by the Capella della Spina, which was built in 1230. Legend claims that some thirty years afterward, a rich Pisan merchant brought the relic back from the Holy Land. However, when he suffered a reversal of fortunes, he fled the city, leaving the fragment in the custody of the Longhi family until 1333, when it was donated to the church and enshrined in a silver reliquary in the form of a tabernacle. Today, it is retained in the chapel of a hospital formerly associated with the church.

Certainly, the thorns were prolific. One investigator enumerated more than seventy. There are reportedly thorns at the Cathedral of Barcelona, St. Michael's Church in Ghent, Spedali Riuniti di S. Chiara in Pisa, Santa Croce in Gerusalemme in Rome, Stanbrook Abbey in England, and elsewhere. Five are on display at the Cathedral of Oviedo, Spain (whose major relic is allegedly one of Jesus' burial cloths, discussed in chapter 10). They are visible behind a circle of glass in their reliquary: a cross held aloft by two angels (Cruz 1984, 34–37).

The Holy Garments

After Jesus was mocked, all four Gospels agree, he was dressed again in his own clothes and led away to be crucified. Writes John (19:23–24):

> Then the soldiers, when they had crucified Jesus, took his garments, and made four parts, to every soldier a part; and also his coat: now the coat was without seam, woven from the top throughout.
>   They said therefore among themselves, "Let us not rend it, but cast lots for it, whose it shall be": that the scripture might be fulfilled, which saith, "They parted my raiment among them, and for my vesture they did cast lots." These things therefore the soldiers did.

The scripture referred to is Psalms 22:18: "They part my garments among them, and cast lots upon my vesture." In *The Life of Jesus,* Craveri (1967, 414) notes that Roman custom dictated that the spoils be divided. "The colorful detail that the legionnaires drew lots to settle the matter," he adds, may be simply "an invention of the Evangelists," intended to cause the supposed prophecy to be fulfilled.

If the Gospel writers were engaging in mythmaking, so were the subsequent relic mongers, who happily supplied the "actual" items that confirmed the myths, and the raconteurs, who contrived pious stories to support them. This appears to be the case with the various holy garments, including two that claim to be the coat "without seam" mentioned by the evangelists. One of these is held by the parish church at Argenteuil, France. The earliest document referring to its existence is the *Charta Hugonis,* written in 1156. However, this states that the church treasury preserved the *Cappa pueri Jesu* (garment of the Child Jesus), which was transformed into the holy coat by a legend that the Blessed Virgin wove for Jesus a garment that miraculously grew as he grew and was therefore worn by him his entire life. (See *Catholic Encyclopedia* 1910, s.v. "Holy Coat.")

Other than the document of 1156, there is only a claim that Empress Irene of Constantinople presented the garment to Charlemagne, emperor of the Holy Roman Empire, in about 800. Charlemagne is said to have given it to his daughter, Theocrate, who was abbess of Argenteuil. Be that as it may, the salient point is that there is no record of the Argenteuil garment that even suggests its historical existence until centuries after Jesus' coat was in the hands of unknown Roman soldiers.

Usually described as a tunic, the Argenteuil garment is reportedly of wine-colored (or variegated) wool and is indeed seamless. There are claims that it bears spots of blood supposedly verified by "scientific analysis," but experience with such reports makes one hesitant to accept them uncritically. As we saw with the "blood" of St. Januarius in chapter 2, and as reiterated in chapter 11, things are not always as they seem in the case of supposedly scientifically authenticated blood relics. Of course, even the existence of real blood spots would not authenticate the tunic of Argenteuil, since it would be a simple matter for a faker to add a few drops of blood for realistic effect.

A rival claim to authenticity attends a garment in the Cathedral of Trier, Germany. Behind the claim is a "venerable tradition" that Queen Helena bequeathed Jesus' robe to the cathedral (Cruz 1984, 23; Thiede and d'Ancona 2002, 27). Unfortunately, the holy coat of Trier is bereft of any documentation that would establish its provenance. Its first artistic depiction is a fifth- or sixth-century ivory tablet that shows relics being transferred to Trier with the aid of Helena.

In 1196 the holy coat of Trier was moved from a chapel to the cathedral's high altar, where it remained undisturbed for more than three centuries. In 1512 it was displayed at a special event in the city. Upon retrieving it from its place of repose, the archbishop and clergy discovered it in a closed chest. It bore an Episcopal seal together with the words, "This is the Seamless Garment of our Lord and Saviour Jesus Christ." Over the succeeding centuries, it was occasionally hidden elsewhere for safekeeping during wartime. It was reportedly given an "archaeological examination" in 1890–1891, but it was obviously not subjected to scientific analysis. We are told vaguely that it was "to all appearances linen or cotton" (*Catholic Encyclopedia* 1910, s.v. "Holy Coat").

The garment was exhibited only three times in the twentieth century, the last time in 1996, the eight-hundredth anniversary of its placement in the high altar. Andrew Gray describes it as a "1.5-yard long and one-yard wide brown garment" and adds:

> The robe, which has been greatly altered over the years and now contains sections of taffeta and silk, was dipped in a rubber solution in a 19th century attempt to preserve it.
> Experts say this makes carbon dating of the few remaining original fragments impossible. (Gray 1996)

Apologists attempt to reconcile the Trier and Argenteuil garments. Each church accepts the authenticity of the other's garment but simply questions which garment it is. Argenteuil advocates believe that theirs is the true seamless garment and that Trier has instead Christ's outer garment (the one touched by the woman who sought healing, referred to in Mark 5:28–30). Conversely, Trier partisans insist that the Argenteuil relic is not the *Tunica inconsutilis* (the seamless tunic) but rather the *Cappa pueri Jesu* discussed earlier. (See *Catholic Encyclopedia*, 1910, s.v. "Holy Coat.")

A major apologist, Joan Carroll Cruz (1984, 27) concludes, with noteworthy credulity: "While it is true that no official records have been found concerning the authenticity of the garments of Trier and Argenteuil from the time of the Crucifixion until the time of St. Helena, still their revered traditions and their documented histories from ancient times go far to confirm the probability of their genuineness." Actually, the lack of a record is worse than she characterizes it.

Nevertheless, both cloths attract pilgrims. The 1996 display of the Trier garment was a boon to local shops that sold T-shirts, coffee mugs, and other souvenirs imprinted with the image of the (formerly) seamless garment (Knuehl 1996). However, a group with an antireligious bent countered with an alternative event: the exhibition of the underwear (or, more accurately, the *alleged* underwear) of a famous resident of Trier, Karl Marx (Gray 1996).

Speaking of undergarments, one German church boasts of having the actual loincloth that Jesus wore on the cross. It is preserved in the Cathedral of Aachen, also known as the Aix La Chapelle (in French) and "the shrine that Charlemagne built." Little is known of the cloth. However, its claim of genuineness can be measured by the fact that the cathedral also purports to preserve the swaddling cloth of the baby Jesus and the reputed shroud of the Virgin Mary (Cruz 1984, 65).

The Lance of Longinus

Before the crucified Jesus died, according to the Gospel of John (19:28–29), he stated, "I thirst," and was given vinegar, administered with a sponge on the end of a reed. (John notes that this fulfilled a scriptural prophecy: "In my thirst they gave me vinegar to drink"

[Psalms 69:21].) Both the sponge and the vinegar were venerated in Jerusalem, although the earliest record of this is from the sixth century. Today, four Roman churches have reputed fragments of that holy sponge, along with one in France. The reed was supposedly divided into four portions, which are now venerated at as many far-flung locations (Cruz 1984, 44).

At nighttime, during crucifixions, Roman law required the legionaries to perform the *crurifragium*, the breaking of the crucified victims' legs. This was done so that no one could, under cover of darkness, set free someone who was still alive (Craveri 1967, 417). However, according to the Gospel of John (19:33–34), "when they [the soldiers] came to Jesus, and saw that he was dead already, they broke not his legs: But one of the soldiers with a spear pierced his side, and forthwith came there out blood and water."

Christian legend makers gave that legionary a name: Longinus. However, there is evidence that it was a made-up name; it derives from a Greek word for lance and simply means "the lancer" (Craveri 1967, 417–18). Somehow, someone later discovered that Longinus' "real" name was Cassius, and it was used by the "visionary" Anne Catherine Emmerich (1904, 197–98):

> The archers still appeared doubtful whether Jesus was really dead, and the brutality they had shown in breaking the legs of the thieves made the holy women tremble as to what outrage they might next perpetrate on the body of our Lord. But Cassius, the subaltern officer, a young man of about five-and-twenty, whose weak squinting eyes and nervous manner had often excited the derision of his companions, was suddenly illuminated by grace, and being quite overcome at the sight of the cruel conduct of the soldiers, and the deep sorrow of the holy women, determined to relieve their anxiety by proving beyond dispute that Jesus was really dead. The kindness of his heart prompted him, but unconsciously to himself he fulfilled a prophecy. He seized his lance and rode quickly up to the mound on which the Cross was planted, stopped just between the cross of the good thief and that of our Lord, and taking his lance in both hands, thrust it so completely into the right side of Jesus that the point went through the heart, and appeared on the left side.

Emmerich next follows the Gospel account but then becomes even more piously imaginative (albeit following a medieval tradition):

> When Cassius drew his lance out of the wound a quantity of blood and water rushed from it, and flowed over his face and body. This species of washing produced effects somewhat similar to the vivifying waters of Baptism: grace and salvation at once entered his soul. He leaped from his horse, threw himself upon his knees, struck his breast, and confessed loudly before all his firm belief in the divinity of Jesus.

Wonders never cease. Continuing to follow a medieval legend, Emmerich then relates that Cassius, who had been partially blind, had his eyesight instantly and miraculously restored.

Longinus' spear became known as the Holy Lance, among other appellations, after it was supposedly found by St. Helena with other relics in the Holy Sepulchre. As we have seen, this was either a treasure trove of the Passion or a convenient discovery site for one fake relic after another. Be that as it may, there is no record of the lance until 570, when a pilgrim reported seeing it in Jerusalem (Cruz 1984, 44).

As with so many other reputed relics, the Holy Lance proliferated. Protestant leader John Calvin (1543, 63), discussing a litany of fakes, stated, "Then follows the iron spear with which our Saviour's side was pierced. It could be but one, and yet by some extraordinary process it seems to have been multiplied into four; for there is one at Rome, one at the Holy Chapel [Sainte Chapelle] at Paris, one at the abbey of Tenaille in Saintonge [France], and one at Selve, near Bourdeaux." Others appeared at Nuremberg, Antioch, Krakow, and Vienna. Cruz (1984, 45) states, "If any staff seems the most valid it would undoubtedly be that which has been honored at St. Peter's Basilica." It is attended by a statue of St. Longinus. However, no such Holy Lance was seen until the sixth century, when pilgrims reported the relic in Jerusalem. Even Cruz (1984, 45) admits, "None of these lances withstands historical scrutiny."

Yet the Holy Lance in Vienna—in the Treasure House of the Hofburg, the former imperial palace—has received considerable attention in modern times. Actually known as the Maurice Spear or

.

the Lance of St. Maurice, it is the subject of an "astonishing legend" (Ravenscroft 1982, 13). Supposedly it came into the possession of Maurice (or Mauritius), a third-century commander of a Christian Roman legion. For refusing to worship Roman pagan deities, he and his legion were allegedly martyred by the tyrannical Maximian. The tale is related in the pseudohistorical *The Spear of Destiny* by Trevor Ravenscroft (1982, 14), which confuses legend, speculation, and fact:

> Altogether 6,666 Legionaries—the most highly disciplined force in Roman military history—divested themselves of their weapons and knelt to bare their necks for slaughter. Maximian made the dreadful decision to massacre the whole legion as an offering of sacrifice to his Gods—the most terrifying single rite of human sacrifice in the history of the ancient world.

Scholars doubt the scope of such a massacre but acknowledge that Maurice and some of his companions were executed (Coulson 1958, 328).

According to Ravenscroft (1982, 10–21), the spear was actually the Spear of the Holy Grail (see figure 6.3). It allegedly passed through history in the possession of successive leaders, including Constantine, King Arthur, Charlemagne, Frederick the Great, and others—forty-five emperors in all. Ravenscroft (1982, 12, 16) asserts that Adolf Hitler was "excited" and "utterly fascinated" by the lance. It and other Hofburg treasures fell into the custody of the Nazis when they invaded Austria in 1938. Recovered by the Americans at the end of World War II, the spear allegedly fascinated General George S. Patton, who removed "the ancient talisman of power" from its leather case and held it in his hands (Ravenscroft 1982, 349–50). Others, however, observe that there is no proof that Patton ever handled the alleged relic of the Crucifixion (*Spear of Jesus* 2004). The United States returned the spear to the Hofburg.

In June 2003, the Spear of Longinus, a.k.a. the Holy Lance, the Spear of Destiny, and other appellations, was subjected to scientific examination. The lance—which now consists of two segments conjoined by a silver sheath—also is bound with a reputed nail from the

Figure 6.3. One of the reputed holy lances—the spear of Longinus—is depicted on the cover of this popular, pseudo-historical account of its alleged peregrinations (author's collection).

True Cross, held in place by threads of copper, silver, and gold. The spear's shape and form were compared with those of known artifacts from the historical period. It was swabbed and tested for organic material (especially blood). The lance was also subjected to x-ray fluorescence and x-ray diffraction tests to determine its composition and structure, along with other nondestructive analyses. The nail was found to be consistent in size and shape with a Roman nail from the first century. The lance was determined not to be a Nazi reproduction, as had been rumored. No trace of organics was found on it. The golden outer sheath was found to date probably from the fourteenth century, and the actual blade was from the seventh or eighth century. In short, the Holy Lance is no such thing; it is merely another fake that has deceived people for centuries. Hollywood continued the fantasy when the "Spear of Destiny" was featured, in faithful mock-up, in the 2005 movie *Constantine*.

CHAPTER 7

Holy Shrouds

Among the most revered—and disputed—relics of the Passion are those associated with the burial of Jesus. Such relics include bits of the angel's candle that lit Jesus' tomb and the marble slab on which his body was laid, complete with traces of his mother's tears (Nickell 1998, 52); most, however, are burial linens. This chapter examines Jewish burial practices, the various alleged winding sheets of Jesus, the controversial Holy Shroud of Constantinople, and what are known as liturgical shrouds.

Jesus' Jewish Burial

The synoptic Gospels are in agreement about Jesus' burial but give scant information. The Gospel of Mark, believed to be the first written, states that Joseph of Arimathea requested and received custody of Jesus' body: "And he bought fine linen, and took him down, and wrapped him in the linen, and laid him in the sepulcher" (Mark 15:46). Luke (23:53) follows Mark almost verbatim, and Matthew (27:59) states that the body was wrapped "in a clean linen cloth."

For "linen" or "linen cloth," the synoptics use the ancient Greek word *sindon*, a linen cloth that could be used for a garment, shroud, or other purpose. For instance, *sindon* is used to describe the garment worn (like a robe) by the "young man" who fled Gethsemane at Jesus' arrest (Mark 14:51–52). In the Septuagint (the Greek translation of the Hebrew Old Testament), Samson uses the word to describe a linen garment worn with a coat or a tunic (Judges 14:12). Toward the end of the first century, a tunic, possibly with a *sindon* wrapped around it, was used for burial by Coptic Christians in Egypt. The body was then wound with ribbons of cloth, like a mummy. In a collection of such burial tunics in the Louvre in Paris are some facecloth-size linens, which are significant in light of the Gospel of John (Wilcox 1977, 60–62; Nickell 1998, 31–32), which provides the fullest account of Jesus' burial (19:38–42):

> Joseph of Arimathea, being a disciple of Jesus, but secretly for fear of the Jews, besought Pilate that he might take away the body of Jesus: and Pilate gave him leave. He came therefore, and took the body of Jesus.
>
> And there came also Nicodemus, which at the first came to Jesus by night, and brought a mixture of myrrh and aloes, about an hundred pound weight.

These spices (Mark refers to "sweet spices" and Luke to "spices and ointments") were used to embalm the body. (See figure 7.1.)

First, however, the body was ritually washed. (This issue becomes important in the discussion of the Shroud of Turin image in chapter 9.) Both the washing and the anointing are expressly mandated by the Jewish Mishnah (Humber 1978, 62). In Acts 9:37 we find a mention of the ritualistic preburial washing of the deceased.

John continues:

> Then took they the body of Jesus, and wound it in linen clothes with the spices, as the manner of the Jews is to bury.
>
> Now in the place where he was crucified there was a garden: and in the garden a new sepulcher, wherein was never man yet laid.
>
> There laid they Jesus therefore because of the Jews' preparation day; for the sepulcher was nigh at hand.

Note John's use of the plural "clothes"—another important issue in the question of the authenticity of the Shroud of Turin.

When the tomb is later found empty, John again refers in the plural to "linen clothes." He says that Simon Peter and "the other disciple, whom Jesus loved," came to the entrance; then Peter "went

Figure 7.1. The burial of Jesus is described most fully in the Gospel of John (19:38–42), on which this depiction is based (mid-nineteenth-century illustration by Julius Schnorr von Carolsfeld).

into the sepulcher, and seeth the linen clothes lie, and the napkin, that was about his head, not lying with the linen clothes, but wrapped together in place by itself" (John 20:6–7). John clearly refers to multiple burial garments, using the plural *othonia*. These are generally understood by biblical scholars to be "strips of linen cloth" or "wrappings" or "linen bandages," indicating that the body was wrapped mummy style. According to one scholarly source, the "bandages" would be "wound fold upon fold round the body" (Dummelow 1951, 808). Some believed that the *sindon*, or sheet, was torn into strips for this purpose (Wilson 1979, 57–58). Another possibility is that *othonia* could include a *sindon*, wound mummy style with ribbons of cloth (as in the case of Coptic burials). Although Luke uses the singular *sindon*, he later reports (24:12) that upon coming to the empty tomb, Peter "beheld the linen clothes laid by themselves." Luke here uses the plural *othonia*, thus reinforcing John's account.

We know that various burial garments were used by the early Christians. According to Pierre Barbet (1950, 161):

> The custom of the first Christians, which must have been inspired by that of the Jews, is confirmed for us by the *Acta Martyrum*, where we always find references to shrouds, linen fabrics, plain linen garments or others more or less ornamented. . . . In the *loculi* of the catacombs one finds linen cloths, cloths dyed purple, figured and ornamented fabrics and silks, cloth of gold and precious garments, such as those in which St. Cecilla is clothed in the cemetery of Domitilla.

Returning to the "napkin" mentioned by John, he employs the Greek word *sudarium* ("sweat cloth"), that is, a handkerchief or napkin (reminiscent of the Coptic facecloth-size linens mentioned earlier). That the *sudarium* refers to the face veil is clear from John's statement that the napkin "was about his [Jesus'] head"; also, in describing the burial of Lazarus, John (11:44) notes, "his face was bound about with a napkin." John states that Jesus was buried "as the manner of the Jews is to bury," and the *sudarium* was used in ancient Jewish practice (Nickell 1998, 33).

The weave of such burial linens was almost certainly plain (unlike, for instance, that of the Shroud of Turin, which is a complex herringbone pattern). Most linens of Jesus' time—whether Roman, Egyptian, or Palestinian—were of a plain weave. States David Sox, "All of the extant Palestinian linen, including the wrappings from the Dead Sea Scrolls, is a regular weave" (quoted in Brown 1981, 31).

Holy Winding Sheets

Regarding the fate of Jesus' burial wrappings, John Calvin (1543, 67) observed, "the evangelists do not mention that either of the disciples or the faithful women who came to the sepulcher had removed the clothes in question, but, on the contrary, their account seems to imply that they were left there." Surely the Gospel writers would not have omitted mentioning that the *othonia* were saved—if indeed

they were. Yet there is no mention of a shroud of Jesus being preserved, nor of one being discovered by St. Helena in the Holy Sepulchre, where she allegedly found the True Cross and so many other
reputed relics of the Passion.

Nevertheless, certain apocryphal texts later claimed that Christ's
othonia had been preserved. The apocryphal writers made many such
additions. For example, to rectify the embarrassment of Christ ap-
pearing after his resurrection to some of his disciples but not to his
mother, some apocryphal texts (including Pseudo-Justin and Acts of
Thaddeus) "remedied this serious oversight of the canonical Gospels" (Craveri 1967, 424).

Hence, in the now-lost second-century Gospel according to the
Hebrews (in a fragment quoted by St. Jerome), it was said that Jesus
himself had presented his *sindon* to the "servant [puero] of the
priest." Some took *puero* to be an error for *Petro* and supposed that
Peter had received the cloth. A fourth-century account mentioned
that Peter had kept the *sudarium*, although what subsequently became of it was unknown. The narrator (St. Nino) alleged that the
burial linen had been obtained by none other than Pilate's wife. This
then passed to Luke, who supposedly hid it away—but neglected to
mention that fact in his Gospel. Another account (about 570) averred
that the *sudarium* was in a cave convent on the Jordan River, even
though the anonymous chronicler had not viewed it himself.

Approximately a century later, a French bishop, Arculf of Péri-
gueux, was shipwrecked near the island of Iona (off the coast of Scotland) and reported seeing a shroud of Jesus on the island. Arculf spun
a tale about how this shroud had been stolen by a converted Jew,
subsequently fell into the possession of infidel Jews, and was finally
claimed by Christians—with an Arab ruler judging the dispute. He
subjected the cloth to trial by fire, whereupon it rose into the air,
unscathed, and fell at the feet of the Christians, who placed it in a
church. According to the credulous Arculf, the shroud was "about
eight feet long" (Wilson 1979, 94; Nickell 1998, 53).

A shroud of the same length surfaced in 877 and was presented
by Charles the Bald to the St. Cornelius Abbey in Compiègne, France.

This Holy Shroud of Compiègne was venerated for more than nine centuries—being the object of great pilgrimages and many state occasions—before perishing in the French Revolution.

A rival shroud was taken in 1098 as crusaders' booty from Antioch to Cadouin. It was revered as the Holy Shroud for centuries and survived the French Revolution, only to be proved a fake in 1935. The Holy Shroud of Cadouin, it turned out, was of eleventh-century origin, its ornamental bands actually consisting of Kufic writing bestowing Muslim blessings (Wilson 1979, 94–95).

Also in the eleventh century, *othonia* of Christ were listed among the relics kept at the emperor's palace in Constantinople. In 1201 these were described by the patriarch of Constantinople, Nicholas Mesarites, as still fragrant with the myrrh used in the anointing of Jesus' body. The cloths were said to have been "of linen, a cheap material, such as was available." To explain their excellent state of preservation, Mesarites claimed, "they have defied decay because they enveloped the ineffable, naked, myrrh-covered corpse after the Passion" (quoted in Humber 1978, 78).

Over the centuries, there have been some forty-three "True Shrouds" of Christ in medieval Europe alone (Humber 1978, 78). John Calvin, in his *Treatise on Relics* (1543, 66), decries the "wicked impostures set up to deceive the public by the pretense that they were each the real sheet in which Christ's body had been wrapped."

For nearly twelve centuries, such reputed burial garments had not borne any image of Jesus' body. However, in 1203 a French crusader may have encountered such a cloth in Constantinople. The Holy Shroud of Constantinople (discussed in the next section) was apparently divided into pieces and distributed in Europe. A century and a half later, another putative *sindon*, now known as the Shroud of Turin, surfaced in Lirey, France. It has been the subject of controversy and even scandal that continue to this day (see chapter 8).

Yet another alleged *sindon*, the Holy Shroud of Besançon (see figure 7.2), appeared in that French city as early as 1523. Proof is lacking that it existed before that time (Panofsky 1953, 364–65); indeed, it was obviously "a mere sixteenth-century copy of that at Turin"

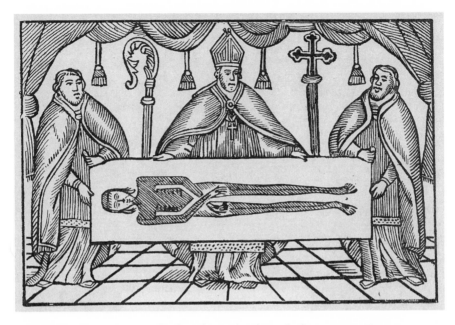

Figure 7.2. Ecclesiastics display the Holy Shroud of Besançon, France (engraving, circa seventeenth century).

(Wilson 1979, 300). Like the Holy Shroud of Compiègne, it was destroyed during the French Revolution.

Shroud of Constantinople

In 1203, a French crusader named Robert de Clari visited the Church of St. Mary of Blachernae in Constantinople, "where was kept the *sydoine* [sic] in which Our Lord had been wrapped, which stood up straight every Friday so that the features of Our Lord could be plainly seen there. And no one, either Greek or French, ever knew what became of this *sydoine* after the city was taken" (quoted in McNeal 1936, 112). Although some understood Robert to be describing a shroud with a body imprint, an authority on his text states: "Robert seems to have confused the *sudarium* (the sweat cloth or napkin, the True Image of St. Veronica) with the *sindon* (the grave cloth in which the body of Jesus was wrapped for entombment). Both relics were in the Church of the Blessed Virgin in the Great Palace, and not in the church in the palace of Blachernae, as Robert says" (McNeal 1936,

112). Not surprisingly, there are other instances of the confusion between the *sudarium* and the *sindon* (Nickell 1998, 54, 55).

Regarding the image on the cloth, Robert de Clari's word translated above as "features" is the Old French "figure"; whether it carried the modern connotation of "face" is debatable. So is the question of whether Robert himself actually saw the cloth. Wilson (1979, 169) argues that he did, but Humber (1978, 79) seems nearer the truth when he notes that, since Robert arrived with the crusaders, "it would seem that he did not see the relic with his own eyes." Humber's view gains support from Robert's confusing the *sudarium* (face-cloth) with the *sindon* (shroud).

Robert de Clari's statement that the cloth "stood up straight every Friday" might suggest a trick, much like the one the same church effected with its alleged Virgin's robe. The robe "was made to appear and miraculously part to reveal an icon of the Virgin beneath," and "it would have been a shrewd psychological move to display the cloth to the superstitious Byzantines for the first time, just as the Virgin's robe was displayed" (Wilson 1979, 169–70). One theorist, Dr. John Jackson, has described how the cloth—if it indeed bore a full-length figure—could have been wound around a batten for this purpose. It could then be lifted by a mechanical device so that the imaged cloth seemed "to raise itself jack-in-the-box style from its casket in exactly the manner Robert de Clari reported of what he saw at the church of St. Mary at Blachernae" (Wilson 1998, 156).

In any event, Robert de Clari could not say whatever became of the cloth. In 1204 the crusaders launched a determined attack on Constantinople. The Byzantines' resistance was soon overcome, the walls were breached near the Blachernae church area, and crusaders streamed into the city. Sacred items were trampled, treasures looted, and wine cellars broken into, whereupon drunken Christian crusaders perpetrated further outrages in the name of religion, representing "one of the most shameful episodes in Western history" (Wilson 1979, 171). (See figure 7.3.)

Although the fate of the Holy Shroud of Constantinople is un-

Figure 7.3. Crusaders desecrated the churches in Constantinople and looted them of holy relics (from *Proctor's History of the Crusades*).

known, we do know that alleged pieces of it were distributed through-out Germany and France. One portion was retained for a time at Constantinople before passing in 1247 to the king of France, who then divided it into smaller parts to be exchanged for other relics (Humber 1978, 79).

Although it is clear (and will become clearer in the following chapter) that the Shroud of Constantinople was not the Shroud of Turin, Robert de Clari's description might have suggested the cre-ation of such a shroud imprinted with Christ's body. Or a later French artist might have gotten the idea of producing an image-laden, double-length shroud, like the Turin one, from other sources—including artistic ones.

Shrouds in Art and Liturgy

The concept of what Jesus' burial garments, or *othonia*, should look like evolved in art. As noted earlier, the synoptic Gospels are vague on this issue, and John's more specific account is open to interpretation. In addition, knowledge of ancient Jewish burial practices dimmed over the centuries in Byzantium and Europe.

Thus, the earliest depictions of Christ's burial showed a mummy-style method of wrapping the body, consistent with that of Lazarus (John 11:44) and Jesus (John 19:40, 20:5–7). When shrouds were depicted, they tended to be only a little longer than a body (approximately eight feet long), like the previously mentioned shrouds of Iona (sixth century) and Compiègne (ninth century). By the eleventh century, artists began to represent the use of a double-length cloth, sufficient to go under the body, turn over the head, and cover the front (like the later Shroud of Turin). Such depictions appeared in certain artistic scenes of the Lamentation (a gathering of Jesus' followers grieving over his body after its removal from the cross) and the Deposition (the placing of Christ's body in the tomb), some of which were rendered in fresco (Wilson 1979, 160).

Also important to the discussion of the evolution of depictions of Jesus' shroud are *epitaphioi*, or liturgical cloths, which were symbolic shrouds. The earliest surviving examples are from the thirteenth century, although Wilson (1979, 160) argues that their similarity to shrouds in Lamentation scenes suggests that they may have emerged in the preceding century. Similar ceremonial shrouds, he notes, remain in use in the Eastern Orthodox Church, covering Christ's ceremonial bier in Good Friday processions. Images on the ceremonial shrouds were full-length depictions of the dead Christ with his hands crossed over the loins. These were typically embroidered onto linen (Sox 1978, 57; Wilson 1979, 160–61).

In addition to artistic depictions and ceremonial shrouds, there is a third source that has relevance to Christ's *othonia*. From the twelfth and thirteenth centuries came exaggerated accounts of the so-called True Image (or veronica). It was claimed that Christ had imprinted not merely his face but the length of his body on white linen cloth. Veronica's Veil was sometimes termed the *sudarium* (facecloth), including in at least two references in the twelfth century (Wilson 1979, 109). The same word was used by John to describe the cloth that covered Jesus' face in the tomb. But we have already seen that the burial *sudarium* was sometimes confused with the *sindon*.

With all these cloths came a merging of traditions: blank, double-length linen holy shrouds (shown in art since the eleventh century) on the one hand, and whole-figured nonshroud linen cloths (liturgical shrouds) from the thirteenth century on the other hand, plus the twelfth- and thirteenth-century veronicas. These were combined and extended in the Shroud of Turin into a "real" shroud with both a front and a back image of Christ's body. That concept was then copied to produce the Shroud of Besançon. In 1624, I. I. Chifflet published his history of Jesus' burial linens, *De Linteis Sepulchralibus Christi, Servatori's Crisis Historica*. He regarded the Shroud of Turin as having wrapped Christ's body *ante pollincturam*—prior to the performance of full burial rites—"thus enabling [Chifflet] to recognize the Besançon Shroud as also authentic" (Wilson 1998, 294).

CHAPTER 8

The Shroud of Turin

The Shroud of Turin is rarely on display, but in 2004 I visited the Cathedral of St. John the Baptist in Turin, Italy, where the cloth is kept (see figure 8.1), as well as the nearby shroud museum (see figure 8.2), which contains a wealth of information (albeit presented from a pro-authenticity perspective) concerning the veronicas, shrouds, and related topics.

This alleged burial cloth of Jesus has a controversial history. I begin this chapter by describing the first appearance of the Shroud of Turin, including the scandalous affair at Lirey, France, when a forger reportedly confessed that it was his handiwork. I then trace its subsequent journey before turning to an examination of the cloth as the reputed shroud of a crucified man. Chapter 9 specifically examines the image on the shroud, chapter 10 discusses an alleged companion cloth, and chapter 11 delves into the reputed blood of Jesus.

The Affair at Lirey

The cloth now known as the Holy Shroud of Turin (see figure 8.3) made its first recorded appearance in north-central France in the middle of the fourteenth century. This occurred at the small provincial town of Lirey in the diocese of Troyes, a short distance southeast of Paris. The exact date is uncertain, but it must have been sometime between 1353, the date a church was established there, and 1357,

(Above) Figure 8.1. The author stands before the container where the Shroud of Turin reposes, surmounted by an enlarged photo of its facial image (author's collection).

(Left) Figure 8.2. Museo della Sindone (Museum of the Shroud) in Turin provides extensive information on myriad aspects of the controversial cloth (author's collection).

Figure 8.3. The Shroud of Turin, being carried
aloft by angels, is depicted in this baroque
painting in the chapel of the Museo della
Sindone in Turin (photo by author).

when the shroud was placed on view by the canons of Lirey. The
wooden collegiate church, named Our Lady of Lirey, was founded by
one Geoffroy de Charny, referred to as a "perfect knight"; he is believed to have presented the cloth to the dean of the proposed abbey
at that time. This is by no means certain, and there is no documentary evidence to prove that the church was specifically founded to
enshrine the cloth. We do know, however, that relics often served as
such an impetus (Wilson 1979, 85–90, 192–94).

In any case, pilgrims thronged to exhibitions of the relic, a fourteen-foot length of linen bearing the front and back imprints of a man who had apparently been crucified like Jesus, as related in the Gospels. The cloth was shown at full length and advertised as the "True Burial Sheet of Christ." The event was commemorated by medallions specially struck for the purpose, one of which has survived: it bears the embossed image of the shroud, held between two cope-attired churchmen. A roundel at the lower center depicts the empty sepulchre of the risen Christ, and on either side of it is a shield with the coat of arms of, respectively, Geoffroy de Charny and his second wife, Jeanne de Vergy. This pilgrim's medallion, dredged up from the Seine in Paris, is the earliest record of this particular Holy Shroud (Wilson 1979, 194). Prior to this there were thirteen centuries of silence.

This complete lack of provenance for what would have been, if genuine, the most holy relic in all of Christendom was among the reasons the shroud was questioned at the time of its first exhibition. Another reason was the failure of the evangelists to mention any imprint of Jesus' body on his burial cloth. As a consequence, the bishop of Troyes, Henri de Poitiers, was urged by "many theologians and other wise persons" to launch an investigation. We know of this first investigation from a lengthy report prepared by a successor to Henri, Bishop Pierre d'Arcis. Writing to Pope Clement VII (the first of the Avignon popes during the great schism), d'Arcis (1389) begins:

> The case, Holy Father, stands thus. Some time since in this diocese of Troyes the Dean of a certain collegiate church, to wit, that of Lirey, falsely and deceitfully, being consumed with the passion of avarice, and not from any motive of devotion but only of gain, procured for his church a certain cloth cunningly painted, upon which by a clever sleight of hand was depicted the twofold image of one man, that is to say, the back and front, he falsely declaring and pretending that this was the actual shroud in which our Savior Jesus Christ was enfolded in the tomb.

D'Arcis continues:

> This story was put about not only in the kingdom of France, but, so to speak, throughout the world, so that from all parts people came together to view it. And further to attract the multitude so that money

might cunningly be wrung from them, pretended miracles were
worked, certain men being hired to represent themselves as healed
at the moment of the exhibition of the shroud, which all believed
to be the shroud of our Lord.

According to d'Arcis, Bishop Henri had become aware of these deceptions and had been "urged by many prudent persons to take action as
indeed was his duty in the exercise of his ordinary jurisdiction."
Henri's investigation was thorough, as d'Arcis observes in his report
to Pope Clement: "Eventually, after diligent inquiry and examination, he discovered the fraud and how the said cloth had been cunningly painted, the truth being attested by the artist who had painted
it, to wit, that it was a work of human skill and not miraculously
wrought or bestowed." Consequently, Bishop Henri took action:

> Accordingly, after taking mature counsel with wise theologians
> and men of the law, seeing that he neither ought nor could allow
> the matter to pass, he began to institute formal proceedings against
> the said Dean and his accomplices in order to root out this false
> persua-sion. They, seeing their wickedness discovered, hid away
> the said cloth so that the Ordinary could not find it, and they kept
> it hidden afterwards for thirty-four years or thereabouts down to
> the present year.

If we subtract d'Arcis's thirty-four years from "the present year"—
1389—we arrive at a date of 1355 or "thereabouts" for the first exhibition and resulting investigation.

However, in 1389 the shroud was brought out of its hiding place
and once again placed on exhibition. In this instance, we understand
why the bishop was bypassed: Bishop d'Arcis was well aware of the
previous scandal and investigation and, as a man of integrity, would
have forbidden the exhibition of a spurious relic. As a result, the dean
of Lirey and its patron, the second Geoffroy de Charny (son of the
first), took action. Bypassing d'Arcis, they went over his head to the
cardinal legate, whom they apparently deceived. "Without entirely
approving the petition," writes d'Arcis, the cardinal permitted the
cloth to be exhibited. The schemers also downplayed the claim that
the shroud was the true Holy Shroud, and they avoided mentioning

that the cloth was the work of an artist. Instead, they were disingenuous and resorted to circulating false rumors. As d'Arcis reports:

> Although it is not publicly stated to be the true shroud of Christ,
> nevertheless this is given out and noised abroad in private, and so it
> is believed by many, the more so, because, as stated above, it was on
> the previous occasion declared to be the true shroud of Christ, and by
> a certain ingenious manner of speech it is now in the said church
> styled not the *sudarium* [burial cloth] but the *sanctuarium* [relic],
> which to the ears of the common folk, who are not keen to observe
> distinctions, sounds much the same thing.

D'Arcis, clearly a man of conscience, resolved to take action and ordered that the exhibition cease, threatening the dean with excommunication if he persisted. However, the conspirators obtained, apparently under false pretenses, a royal warrant and even a royal honor guard to attend the exhibition. The shroud was displayed on a high platform flanked with torches. D'Arcis countered by approaching King Charles VI and relating the true facts. Charles ordered the cloth seized by the bailiff of Troyes, but the unsuccessful bailiff returned from his mission carrying not the cloth of Lirey but word of the dean's refusal to comply (Wuenschel 1957, 64; Walsh 1963, 53).

In time, Geoffroy applied secretly to Pope Clement, who, without investigating or hearing d'Arcis, imposed silence on the latter. As it happened, Geoffroy de Charny was a close relation of Clement. Geoffroy's mother, the widow Jeanne de Vergy, had shrewdly remarried, her second husband being the pope's wealthy uncle. Nevertheless, despite risks to himself, d'Arcis drafted his lengthy report, recounting the basic facts and defending himself against accusations of jealousy and of desiring to obtain the shroud for himself.

Pierre d'Arcis threw down the gauntlet to the Lirey hawkers: "I offer myself here," he stated, "as ready to supply all information sufficient to remove any doubt concerning the facts alleged both from public report and otherwise." Doubtless, among his "many prudent advisers" (some of whom thought he moved "too half-heartedly in the matter" and made himself "a laughing-stock by allowing the abuse to continue") were persons still living who knew the truth about Bishop Henri de Poitiers' first investigation. However, it was clearly the shroud's owners who were acting deceitfully, because they would not explain how the shroud had come to be in their possession. Wilson (1979, 87) concedes, "the de Charnys' guilt seemed to be independently demonstrated by various factors, not least of which is that they failed to make any attempt to explain how they acquired the cloth. If the shroud was genuine, such an explanation would surely put an end to the matter."

D'Arcis (1389) wrote to Clement that he could not "fully or sufficiently express in writing the grievous nature of the scandal," and he expressed his fear for the "danger to [the] souls" of those misled by "the delusion and scandal." In response, Clement heard the evidence and concluded that the cloth of Lirey was a painted cloth and not a shroud. Although he permitted exhibitions to continue, he placed severe restrictions on them. There could be no candles, incense, or guard of honor. Further, he ordered that whenever the shroud was displayed, it must be loudly announced, "it is not the True Shroud of Our Lord, but a painting or picture made in the semblance or representation of the shroud." On January 6, 1390, Clement signed the documents that effectively settled the matter—for the time being. As noted later in this chapter, there would be further scandals involving the shroud and another generation of de Charnys.

A Confessed Forger

Bishop Pierre d'Arcis claimed that the shroud had been "cunningly painted," a fact "attested by the artist who had painted it." Was Bishop d'Arcis correct? Wilson (1998, 121) assessed the issue of the d'Arcis memorandum's credibility:

> Many pro-Shroud writers have tried to undermine Bishop d'Arcis and his memorandum's credibility. They have criticised his bad temper and his "barbarous" Latin, and they have also pointed out that although there are two copies of the memorandum, neither of these is the original, both being just unsigned, undated drafts.
>
> However, although the latter facts are perfectly genuine, the truth is that whatever d'Arcis's command of Latin, he had held the major

see of Troyes for some twelve years and before then had had a respectable career as a lawyer. Also, whatever his temper at the time, in his memorandum he set out the facts as he knew them with complete lucidity. And there are just too many ancillary supporting documents for these to be in serious dispute.

If d'Arcis's statement about a forger having confessed were untrue, he could have been challenged by the shroud's custodians, yet they maintained what appears to have been a guilty silence. Recall that d'Arcis had stated that he was "ready to supply all information sufficient to remove any doubt concerning the facts alleged." Thus, the bishop's claim stood. Still extant is the report of the bailiff of Troyes, dated 1389, stating that the shroud was a painting (Wuenschel 1957, 64; Walsh 1963, 53). And Pope Clement ultimately judged that it was only a "painting" or "representation" of the shroud.

Who was this artist? Like so many of his fellow craftsmen, his name remains unknown to us. We are aware that he flourished in the 1350s in north-central France, probably living in the diocese of Troyes —possibly even the city of Troyes itself—since he seems to have been quite accessible to the investigating bishop of Troyes.

Although the artist's genius has sometimes been exaggerated, he was certainly a skilled and clever artisan. He did make mistakes, however. He showed ingenuity, study, and skill in many ways, not the least of which was accurately distributing the darks and lights in a manner consistent with a bodily imprint. That he did not include the wraparound distortions that a real body would have left is no doubt attributable to his overriding artistic sensibility.

The traditional way of naming an unknown but important artist is to designate him "Master," followed by an appropriate descriptor —such as a place (Master of Flémalle or Master Honoré de Paris) or a work of art (Master of the Altar of St. Bartholomew or Master of the Castello Nativity). One fifteenth-century engraver is known as the Master of 1466, and a sixteenth-century enameler has been given the designation Master K.I.P. , based on the monograms on his works (Janson 1963, 267–68; Davidson and Gerry 1939, 226–27). Likewise, the tradition for naming a purported shroud is by its place of display, such as the Shroud of Cadouin, the Shroud of Besançon, and the Shroud of Compiègne.

In this light, the title Master of the Shroud of Lirey seems appropriate, since the original place name is the one connected with him historically. That designation also helps de-emphasize the accusation of crass forgery against the artist. Although the cloth was originally misrepresented as the authentic shroud of Jesus, it is far from certain that the artist was initially aware of the intended deception. He could have been commissioned to make a symbolic shroud— albeit an unusually realistic one—for reputedly ceremonial purposes. In any event, such a skilled craftsman must have produced many additional works of art, all of which are part of his implicit legacy.

Journey of the Holy Shroud

In 1418, when war threatened Lirey, the granddaughter of the shroud's original owner, Margaret de Charny, sought to obtain the cloth for safekeeping. She and her husband, a wealthy count named Humbert de Villersexel, obtained permission from the Lirey canons to house the cloth in the Charny castle, known as Montfort. Humbert issued a receipt in his own hand, dated July 6, 1418. It covered various "jewels and relics," including the shroud—fully acknowledged as a painted fake. He described it as "a cloth, on which is the figure or representation of the Shroud of Our Lord Jesus Christ, which is a casket emblazoned with the de Charny crest" (quoted in Wilson 1979, 212).

Humbert's receipt promised that when the hostilities ended (the Hundred Years' War was still devastating France), the jewels and relics would be returned. Instead, the cloth was transferred to a chapel in Humbert's domain, where it remained until his death in 1438. Margaret failed to heed the pleas of the canons of Lirey for the cloth's return, as well as an order from the Parlement of Dôle. She stalled, promised, delayed, and promised some more but ultimately refused to return the cloth. Instead, Margaret took it on tour, where she apparently misrepresented the cloth as genuine and where it encountered various challenges to its authenticity (Nickell 1998, 17–19). Finally, in 1453—although she would be excommunicated for it—

Margaret sold the cloth to the Royal House of Savoy (later the Italian monarchy). Authenticity advocates like to say that Margaret "gave" the cloth to the duke and duchess, which is true, although they "gave" her two castles in return (Nickell 1998, 19).

The shroud was now reputed to have additional powers. According to Wilson (1979, 216), "In the earliest days with the family it was carried about with them on its travels, like a holy charm to safeguard them against the dangers of the journey." In later centuries, the shroud reportedly provided protective powers over whatever city housed it. Yet in 1532 it was unable even to protect itself. It nearly perished in a fire that destroyed the Savoy Chapel at Chambéry, resulting in burn marks and water stains that marred the image.

In a shrewd political move to relocate the Savoy capital, the shroud was taken in 1578 to Turin, where it has remained ever since (except for a period during World War II, when it was lodged in a remote abbey for safekeeping). During the seventeenth century the shroud continued to be exhibited on occasion in Turin. Engravings from this period depict the shroud as a battle standard, waving above the Duke (Amadeus) and Duchess of Savoy and bearing the inscription, "In this sign, conquer."

The shroud continued to be generally regarded as authentic, although the church never proclaimed it as such. But notes of skepticism, or at least extreme caution, were sounded. For example, in Rome in 1670, the Congregation of Indulgences granted to shroud pilgrims a plenary indulgence, "not for venerating the cloth as the true Shroud of Christ, but rather for meditating on his Passion, especially his death and burial" (quoted in Wilson 1979, 221). One wonders whether the Congregation was aware of Clement's 1389 decree, which the indulgence strongly echoed.

On June 1, 1694, the shroud was placed in its present shrine in the Cathedral of St. John the Baptist, a black marble chapel designed by the architect Guarino Guarini (see figure 8.4). At this time, the shroud was provided with a new backing cloth and some additional patches (Hynek 1951, 11; Wilson 1979, 264). The cloth was exhibited only sporadically during subsequent centuries.

Figure 8.4. The Shroud of Turin is housed in the Cathedral of St. John the Baptist (photo by author).

The shroud's modern history began in 1898, when it was first photographed and its double imprints subjected to widespread scrutiny. Its reputed photonegative properties and other features were extensively analyzed and debated. In 1931 better photos were taken.

In 1969 the archbishop of Turin appointed a secret commission to examine the shroud. That fact was leaked and then denied, but "at last the Turin authorities were forced to admit what they had previously denied," and the clerics were accused of acting "like thieves in the night" (Wilcox 1977, 44). More detailed studies—again clandestine—began in 1973. Internationally known forensic serologists made heroic efforts to validate the "blood," but all the microscopic, chemical, biological, and instrumental tests were negative. This was not surprising, given the stains' suspicious redness and picturelike appearance (the "blood" is discussed more fully in chapter 11). An art expert concluded that the image had been produced by an artistic printing

Figure 8.5. Famed microanalyst Walter C. McCrone (1916–2002) discovered tempera paint on the Turin "shroud" (photo by Joseph Barabe, copyright McCrone Scientific Photography).

technique. The commission's report was withheld until 1976 and then was largely suppressed, whereas a rebuttal report was freely available. Thus began an approach that would be repeated over and over: distinguished experts were asked to examine the cloth and were then attacked when they did not obtain the desired results.

Further examinations were conducted in 1978 by the Shroud of Turin Research Project (STURP). STURP consisted of mostly religious believers whose leaders served on the Executive Council of the Holy Shroud Guild, a Catholic organization that advocated the "cause" of the supposed relic. STURP members, like others who called themselves "sindonologists" (or "shroudologists"), gave the impression that they started with the desired answer and worked backward. STURP lacked experts in art and forensic chemistry, with one exception: famed microanalyst Walter C. McCrone (see figure 8.5). Examining samples tape-lifted from the shroud, McCrone determined that the "blood" and image imprints had been done in tempera paint. All these scientific results are examined more fully in chapters 9 and 11.

A Linen Cloth

As noted earlier, the use of a single large cloth to wrap a body for burial is not typical of early Jewish practice and is contrary to the Gospel of John, which refers to multiple cloths, including a separate "napkin" over the face. In addition, whereas ancient burial linens tended to be plain weave, the cloth of Turin is woven in a complex, three-to-one twill, striped in a herringbone pattern. Although shroud advocates point out that such a weave *could* have been made at the time of Jesus, evidence is lacking that it *was*. Somewhat disingenuously, they switch the discussion to twills in general (Antonacci 2000, 99). Wilson (1998, 69) is frank on this issue: "It has to be acknowledged that no actual examples of *linen* directly matching the herringbone twill of the Shroud survive from antiquity, but this is far from saying that examples did not and could not have existed in this fabric."

Textile expert Gilbert Raes, who served on the secret commission mentioned earlier, found traces of cotton among the linen threads and determined it to be of a Middle Eastern variety, indicating that the cloth originated from that part of the world. Wilson (1998, 71) now admits that he and others were misled by Raes' conclusions. There was a flourishing cotton industry in Europe by the thirteenth century; moreover, a French textile expert, Gabriel Vial, observed that the cotton traces may be purely incidental, possibly coming from the cotton gloves of people who handled the shroud. In fact, very few examples of Palestinian cloth exist due to the excessive humidity of the climate (Humber 1978, 35). Yet the shroud appears to be in a rather astonishing state of preservation for its reputed age of nearly two thousand years. According to David Sox (quoted in Brown 1981, 31):

> There are lots of samples much older than 2,000 years. Linen, which is essentially cellulose, is an extremely durable material. But what *is* a problem is that you just don't find anything quite the size of the Shroud except for Egyptian mummy wrappings—certainly nothing that measures fourteen feet, the size of the Shroud. That's a helluva lot of linen! What I'm suggesting is that it's just too large to be convincing, too much to have been kept intact for so long.

The problem of the cloth's survival is magnified by the fact that, as a Christian relic, it would have been the target of both pillaging armies and the Iconoclasts (723–842), who destroyed countless other miraculous "portraits" of Christ. Considering all the evidence, the shroud seems more consistent with an age of six centuries rather than twenty (Nickell 1998, 36).

A curious point of evidence is the "side strip," an eight- to nine-centimeter-wide strip of linen sewn along one edge of the shroud. Of identical weave to the main segment, it appears to have been sewn on approximately contemporaneously with the origin of the shroud. The most likely explanation, argues Wilson (1979, 71), is that it was added "in order to balance the image on the cloth."

A persistent attempt to give the shroud a provenance before its appearance in medieval France was based on the claim of Swiss criminologist Max Frei-Sulzer, who reportedly found certain pollen grains on the cloth that could have come only from plants growing solely in Palestine at the time of Jesus. Earlier, Frei claimed to have discovered pollens on the cloth that were characteristic of Istanbul (formerly Constantinople) and the area of ancient Edessa, seeming to confirm a "theory" about the shroud's missing early history. Wilson (1979, 106–24) conjectured that the shroud was actually the fourth-century image of Edessa, a legendary "miraculous" imprint of Jesus' face made as a gift to King Abgar (see chapter 4). Wilson's notion was that the shroud had been folded so that only the face showed; thus it had been disguised for centuries. Logically, though, had the cloth been kept in a frame for such a long period, there would have been an age-yellowed, rectangular area around the face. Nevertheless, Frei's alleged pollen evidence seemed to give new support to Wilson's ideas.

Frei had severe credibility problems, however. Before his death in 1983, his reputation suffered greatly when, after representing himself as a handwriting expert, he pronounced the infamous "Hitler diaries" genuine. They were soon exposed as forgeries. Meanwhile, an even more serious question had arisen about Frei's pollen evidence. Although he reported finding numerous types of pollen from Palestine and other areas, STURP's tape-lifted samples, taken at the

same time, showed little pollen. Micropaleontologist Steven D. Schafersman was probably the first to publicly suggest that Frei might be
guilty of deception. He explained how unlikely it was, given the evidence of the shroud's exclusively European history, that thirty-three
different Middle Eastern pollens could have reached the cloth—
particularly only pollen from Palestine, Istanbul, and the Anatolian
steppe. Frei's work was also suspect for what was *not* found. He did
not report a single pollen grain from the olive trees that proliferate in
Palestine. With such selectivity, Schafersman stated, "these would
be miraculous winds indeed." In an article in *Skeptical Inquirer*,
Schafersman (1982) called for an investigation of Frei's work.

After Frei's tape samples became available following his death,
McCrone was asked to authenticate them. This he was readily able
to do, he told me, "since it was easy to find red ocher on linen fibers
much the same as I had seen them on my samples." But there were
few pollen grains other than on a single tape, which bore "dozens" in
one small area. This indicated that the tape had subsequently been
"contaminated," probably deliberately, by pulling back the tape and
introducing the pollen surreptitiously. McCrone (1993) added:

> One further point with respect to Max [Frei] which I haven't men-
> tioned anywhere, anytime to anybody is based on a statement made
> by his counterpart in Basel as head of the Police Crime Laboratory
> there that Max had been several times found guilty and was censured
> by the Police hierarchy in Switzerland for, shall we say, overenthusi-
> astic interpretation of his evidence. His Basel counterpart had been
> on the investigating committee and expressed surprise in a letter to
> me that Max was able to continue in his position as Head of the
> Police Crime Lab in Zurich.

That the shroud's cloth dated not to the first century but to the
Middle Ages was reported on October 13, 1988, after samples were
carbon-dated. Postage-stamp-size samples were snipped from one
end of the main portion of the shroud and transferred to laboratories
at Zurich, Oxford, and the University of Arizona. Using accelerator
mass spectrometry, the labs obtained dates in close agreement: the
linen dated from about 1260 to 1390, about the time of the forger's

confession. The results were given added credibility by correct dates obtained on control swatches of ancient cloths (Damon et al. 1989).

But shroud defenders would not accept such results and rushed to challenge the carbon-14 tests. According to Scavone (1989, 104–5):

> They argued that the three labs had been given pieces of cloth taken from a much handled, much contaminated corner of the Shroud. Since only threads were needed, different parts of the Shroud could and should have been included, such as the "pristine" material next to the charred areas under the patches. Another major objection was that all three labs had agreed to use the same newly developed and relatively untested cleansing solvent. Since the contamination from centuries of handling is the most important obstacle to an accurate C-14 date, this procedure seemed to critics to be extremely careless.

Actually, their numerous criticisms of the carbon dating are little more than sour grapes, given the close proximity of the dates obtained from the three labs, the accuracy in dating the control swatches, and the fact that the samples were thoroughly cleansed before testing, along with other reasons that I pointed out in an article commissioned by the prestigious French science magazine *Science et Vie* (Nickell 1991).

Some shroud devotees took a mystical tack, suggesting that the imagined burst of radiant energy at the moment of Christ's resurrection had altered the carbon ratio. Then there was the notion of Russian scientist Dmitrii Kuznetsov, who claimed to have established experimentally that heat from a fire (like that of 1532) could alter the radiocarbon date. Others could not replicate his alleged results, however, and it turned out that his physics calculations had been plagiarized—complete with an error (Wilson 1998, 219–23). (Kuznetsov was also exposed in *Skeptical Inquirer* magazine for bogus research in a study criticizing evolution [Larhammar 1995].)

A more persistent challenge to the radiocarbon testing was hurled by Leoncio Garza-Valdez (1999, 37). He claimed to have obtained a swatch of the "miraculous cloth" that bore a microbial coating, contamination that could have altered the radiocarbon date. That possibility was effectively debunked by physicist Thomas J.

Pickett (1996). He performed a simple calculation showing that, for the shroud's date to have been altered by thirteen centuries (from Jesus' first-century death to the radiocarbon date of 1325, plus or minus 65 years), there would have had to be twice as much contamination, by weight, as the cloth itself.

Still more recently, retired research chemist Ray Rogers, formerly of STURP, tried a new approach. He claimed that traces of cotton and rose madder dye or paint found on cuttings of linen left over from the carbon dating indicated that the samples had come from an "invisible reweave" type of patch, probably done in the Middle Ages. However, textile experts had approved the sample site, and contrary to Rogers' assertion, cotton and madder had been found elsewhere on the cloth. Rogers offered an alternative method of dating, based on the amount of lignin decomposition, which he applied to various leftover shroud samples. He concluded that the shroud was much older than the C-14 date indicated (Rogers 2005a, 2005b). However, that improvised test is not an accepted one, was based on limited samples, was not done in a double-blind manner, and has not been replicated (Nickell 2005).

As we have seen, however, there is corroborative evidence that supports the radiocarbon date of 1260 to 1390. This includes the lack of any history before the 1350s, the reported forger's confession at that time, and certain artistic conventions that likewise point to the fourteenth century. The next chapter provides still more evidence that the Shroud of Turin is the handiwork of a medieval artisan.

CHAPTER 9

"Photograph" of Christ

Despite evidence to the contrary—the Gospel accounts, lack of provenance, forger's confession, suspiciously modern weave and condition of the cloth, and radiocarbon date of 1260 to 1390—many are still convinced that the Shroud of Turin exhibits an authentic imprint of Christ's body. In this chapter I consider the shroud's double image, possible imaging methods, anatomic and medical considerations, and evidence that the image is a work of art.

Image on the Shroud

As Bishop Pierre d'Arcis described it, the shroud bears "the twofold image of one man, that is to say, the back and front." The effect is of a cloth placed under the man's body and folded over the head to cover the front. As we have already seen, this is consistent with neither the Gospel of John nor Jewish burial practices.

The "body" images on the shroud are monochromatic and sepia in color, which some have likened to lightly scorched linen or to the color of the burial spices myrrh and aloes. The excising and cross-sectioning of a limited number of threads have shown that the stain is superficial—not penetrating the cloth but confined to the topmost fibers (Nickell 1998, 80–87, 112; Wilson 1979, 74). The other main type of image on the shroud is that of the "blood," which has remained suspiciously red and picturelike (qualities discussed more fully in chapter 11). (See figure 9.1, right.)

In 1898 the shroud was photographed for the first time, and the glass-plate negatives showed a more lifelike image of a man (as also shown in subsequent photos; for example, see figure 9.1, right). Thus began the modern era of shroud inquiry, with proponents asking how a mere medieval forger could have produced a perfect "photographic" negative before the development of photography. In fact, the analogy with photographic images is misleading: the "positive" image shows a figure with white hair and beard, the opposite of what would be expected of a Palestinian Jew in his thirties. Nevertheless, some shroud advocates suggested that the image was produced by simple contact with bloody sweat or burial ointments. The prominences would therefore be imprinted, while the recesses would remain blank, thus producing quasi-negative images.

The man of the shroud is obviously not some anonymous crucifixion victim. With wounds like those described in the Gospels—pierced hands and feet, scalp bleeding as from a crown of thorns, and lance wound in the side—the figure is obviously either Jesus or an artist's representation of him. (The wounds and other medical evidence and anatomic considerations are discussed later in this chapter.)

The figure's height has been variously estimated, owing to some indistinctness in the area of the feet. Some suggest five feet eleven inches, which Wilson (1979, 35) concedes is "an impressive height." Others suggest six feet or more, a considerable but not impossible height for a first-century Palestinian (Nickell 1998, 72–74).

In addition to the touted photonegativity, the images supposedly exhibit "encoded" three-dimensional properties. Unfortunately, the claims of the Shroud of Turin Research Project (STURP) in this regard were exaggerated; some internal consistency in tonal gradation over localized regions of the image was all it established. Artists have reproduced this so-called three-dimensional effect.

Besides the body imprints and "blood," some shroud enthusiasts claim to discern additional images in photos of the shroud. In smudgy-appearing areas that were subsequently enhanced, they perceive plant

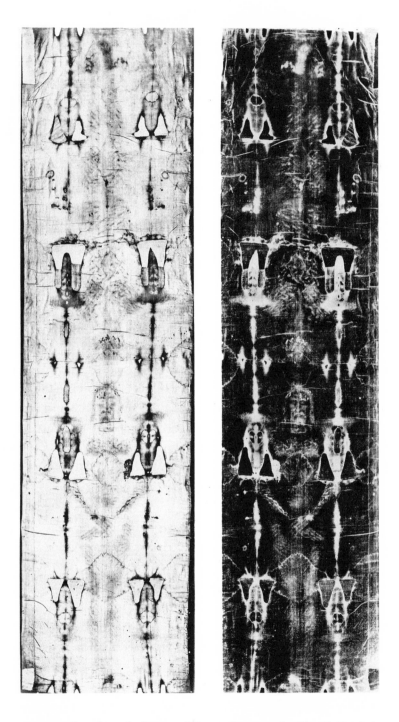

Figure 9.1. The Shroud of Turin: left, as photographed by G. Enrie in 1935; right, as Enrie's photo appears on the negative.

images that supposedly link the European cloth with Palestine. Such work was done by a retired geriatric psychiatrist Alan Whanger and his wife, Mary. They were later assisted by an Israeli botanist who looked at their photos of "flower" images (many of them "wilted" and otherwise distorted) and exclaimed, "Those are the flowers of Jerusalem!" Apparently, no one has thought to see whether some might match the flowers of France or Italy or to try to prove that the images are indeed floral (given the relative scarcity of pollen grains on the cloth).

These flower and plant images join other shapes perceived, Rorschach style, in the shroud's mottled image and off-image areas. These include Roman coins over the eyes; head and arm phylacteries (small Jewish prayer boxes); an amulet; Crucifixion-associated items (compare John 19) such as a large nail, a hammer, a sponge on a reed, a Roman thrusting spear, pliers, two scourges, two brush brooms, two small nails, a large spoon or trowel in a box, a loose coil of rope, a cloak with a belt, a tunic, and a pair of sandals; and other far-fetched imaginings, including Roman dice—all discovered by the Whangers and their botanist friend (Whanger and Whanger 1998).

They and others have also reported finding ancient Latin and Greek words, such as "Jesus" and "Nazareth." Even shroud proponent Ian Wilson (1998, 242) felt compelled to state, "While there can be absolutely no doubting the sincerity of those who make these claims, the great danger of such arguments is that researchers may 'see' merely what their minds trick them into thinking is there."

The Imprinting

It is crucial to observe that no burial cloth in the history of the world has borne images like those of the Shroud of Turin. If they were, in fact, imprints, the laws of geometry would apply; yet there are no wraparound distortions as would be expected if a cloth enclosed a three-dimensional form. Imprints of real faces, which I have produced (Nickell 1998, 80), are necessarily grotesquely distorted.

Then there is the law of gravity. Far less pressure is exerted by a lightweight cloth resting on a body than is exerted by a body resting heavily on a cloth placed under it. In other words, the frontal image should appear noticeably lighter than the dorsal one, and on the dorsal image, areas such as the buttocks should exhibit pressure-point flattening. Yet an official report of STURP acknowledges: "the densities at presumed contact points on both frontal and dorsal images do not differ significantly. These characteristics along with the superficial nature of the image would suggest that the contact transfer mechanism is pressure-independent." The report calls attention to this "apparent contradiction" (Schwalbe and Rogers 1982, 33–35; Nickell 1998, 78–81).

Other shroud theorists recognized that not all the imprinted features would have been in contact with a cloth that was simply draped over a body. Therefore, any imaging process would have had to act across a distance—that is, it must have been *projected* somehow. Thus was born the notion of "vaporography," or the claim that weak ammonia vapors from the fermented urea in sweat interacted with spices on the cloth (likened to a sensitized photographic plate) to create a vapor "photo." Unfortunately, as experiments I conducted in 1977 demonstrated, vapors do not travel in perfectly straight vertical lines. Instead, they diffuse and convect, resulting in a blur (Nickell 1998, 74–84).

Still other shroud proponents invoked a miracle, although they tried to present it in scientific-sounding terms. Certain members of STURP proposed that the image was the result of "flash photolysis" —a supposed short burst of radiant energy such as that envisioned emanating from Christ's body at the moment of his resurrection. In short, the image was thought to be a "scorch picture." One STURP scientist, Ray Rogers, later admitted, "I incline toward the idea of a scorch, but I can't think how it was done. At this point, you either keep looking for the mechanism or start getting mystical" (quoted in Nickell 1998, 93). Reasons for doubting radiation scorching as a mechanism are numerous. For one thing, real scorches on linen (such as those on the shroud resulting from the fire of 1532) exhibit a strong reddish fluorescence, whereas the shroud images do not fluoresce at all. In addition, examination of the cloth's threads show the image stain to be confined to the topmost fibers, and there is no known ra-

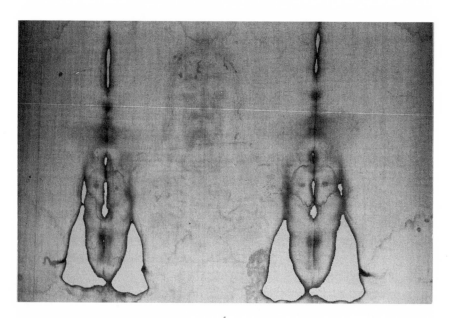

Figure 9.2. The shroud's sepia tones are superficially the color of scorches, but real scorches flanking the image (from the fire of 1532) have different properties (detail from a photoreproduction of the shroud displayed in the chapel of the Museo della Sindone, Turin; photo by author).

diation that—traveling various distances from body to cloth—would act uniformly superficially. Moreover, there is no natural source for any such radiation, and even if there were, there is no means of focusing it to produce an image like that on the shroud (Nickell 1998, 91–94). (See figure 9.2.)

Nevertheless, one shroud enthusiast, writing in William Buckley's conservative *National Review*, suggested that the image had been created by thermonuclear reactions and was analogous to laser-produced holograms (Nickell 1998, 93). Such absurdities led skeptics to joke about "a science of miracles." Indeed, a lawyer who describes himself as "a board member of several Shroud groups" seems to propose just that. Having swept aside any type of artistry as a mechanism, he asserts "that the images of the Shroud literally defy the laws of chemistry and physics as we understand them." His proposed "theory" is that "if a body instantaneously dematerialized or disappeared, particle radiation would be given off naturally and all the unique features found on the Shroud's body images and blood marks would occur" (Antonacci 2000, 245).

Before his death in March 2005, Ray Rogers (2004, 69) dismissed such astonishing nonsense, disparaging what he termed "lunatic fringes" and "religious zealots." He believed that the image was the result of "decomposition products of a rotting body," adding, "No miracles or painters are required." Unfortunately, as we have seen, the lack of wraparound distortions and other evidence rules out the "rotting body" scenario. But what about artists—whom shroud proponents are so eager to dismiss?

Artists have, in fact, produced many comparable images. In 1979 I published the results of my successful experiments in simulating the mysterious images. The method—a rubbing technique using a bas-relief sculpture (to minimize distortion) and powdered pigments (to limit depth of penetration)—automatically yields quasi-negative imprints with numerous points of similarity to the image on the Turin cloth. These include encoded three-dimensional information and numerous other shroud features, some of which specifically point to some form of imprinting technique (Nickell 1998, 101–6). (See figures 9.3 and 9.4.)

Subsequently, microanalyst Walter McCrone determined that the double image had been done in a dilute tempera medium (discussed in detail later). Under his direction, Chicago artist Walter Sanford produced convincing shroudlike images (McCrone 1996, 149). As McCrone's guest at a 1982 microscopy conference, I watched Sanford carefully paint such an image. Except for soaking into the cloth —which could be minimized by using a more "dry-brush" technique —his reproduction was a very credible one.

Forensic anthropologist Emily Craig and Randall Bresee of the University of Tennessee used a method that combined features of McCrone's and my techniques: they applied dry pigments freehand onto a suitable surface, then transferred the image to cloth by rubbing. Their resultant image also exhibited three-dimensional characteristics like those on the Shroud of Turin (*Mysterious Man* 1997). Antonacci (2000, 77) has voiced several complaints about this technique, but they are

Figure 9.3. Negative photograph of the face on the Shroud
of Turin shows a quasi-positive
image—supposedly impossible
for an artist to accomplish
(detail of figure 9.1, right).

specious or based on faulty assumptions. For instance, he claimed that
the Craig-Bresee image lacked the diffuseness and faintness of the
shroud image; however, evidence indicates that the shroud's image
was once much bolder, consistent with pigment having sloughed off
with six hundred years of handling (Nickell 1998, 104).

Various other techniques have been demonstrated or merely
hypothesized, ranging from the sublime to the ridiculous. Among
the latter is the bizarre twist given to the shroud's touted photonegative properties with the publication of Lynn Picknett and Clive
Prince's *Turin Shroud: In Whose Image? The Truth behind the Centuries-Long Conspiracy of Silence* (1994). (These are the same authors whose conspiracy theories regarding Leonardo da Vinci and
the Holy Grail were exposed as nonsense in chapter 3.) This time,
the conspiracy-minded duo's "truth" was the ludicrous notion that
the shroud image was the world's first actual photograph—produced
by Leonardo da Vinci himself. Never mind that Leonardo (1452–1519)
was not even born until a century *after* the shroud first appeared at

Figure 9.4. Negative photograph of an experimental image made by the author—a rubbing from a bas-relief—reveals a shroudlike picture.

Lirey, France, in the mid-1350s, and that the shroud image does not have the properties of an actual photograph (see Nickell 1998, 77–78). Never mind, also, the tempera paint on the image and the fact that Leonardo neglected to record the invention of photography in his celebrated notebooks.

Much of the controversy concerning image formation, and the difficulty in knowing which of the conflicting characteristics reported are correct, must be blamed on the shroud's custodians. Access to the cloth has been consistently refused to skeptics. STURP lacked artists on its team, and its art forgery expert, McCrone, was not permitted access to the actual cloth; he was limited to examining samples taken from the surface fibers at selected sites.

Medical Evidence

For many years, at the forefront of the pro-authenticity argument were those claiming that the shroud image was so anatomically accurate and the "wounds" so realistic and consistent with the pathology of scourging and crucifixion that the imprints must be those of an actual crucified man. Much of this initial work was by a French

Catholic surgeon named Pierre Barbet, the so-called doctor at Calvary. Barbet claimed to be objective, but when another pro-shroud pathologist, Dr. Anthony Sava, obtained some "very contradictory findings," the French doctor invited him to Paris to discuss the issues. Recalls Sava (1977, 54):

> To my utter amazement he asked me not to publish any of my findings because "they were absolutely wrong. Besides, my findings were proven correct by the very wide acceptance by the experts!" He explained further that he had done his experimental work more than twenty years before and he was no longer young and therefore unable to become involved in any revival of controversy. In all kindness to Dr. Barbet, I confess that such an attitude is far from scientific. As I saw it then and still do, truth in such matters is not determined by the degree of public approval nor by the longevity of a belief that unfortunately has a way of becoming enshrined, arbitrary and dogmatic.

Sava (1977, 51) also concluded that Barbet's "personal piety clouded the boundary between subjectivity and scientific medical appraisal."

Barbet was followed by other pro-authenticity pathologists impressed with the anatomic realism and accurate "blood" flows depicted on the shroud—even if these were often interpreted quite differently. In fact, however, there are anatomic flaws. For example, one arm is longer than the other, and the hair falls as if for a standing figure rather than a reclining one. Moreover, the physique is so unnaturally elongated (like figures in Gothic art) that one pro-shroud pathologist concluded that Jesus must have suffered from the rare disease known as Marfan's syndrome, which is characterized by excessively long extremities.

Additional evidence against authenticity is found in the "blood" flows. They are unnaturally picturelike and have remained suspiciously red (among other flaws discussed more fully in chapter 11). Also, the dried "blood," such as that on the arms, demonstrates that the "body" imprinted on the shroud was not washed, although ritual washing was expressly mandated by the Jewish Mishnah.

A considerable challenge to authenticity is the "bloodstained" right footprint of the dorsal image. In order for the foot to leave such a print, the knee must have been bent at a considerable angle, thus raising the calf of the leg a significant distance away from the underlying cloth. Yet the calf of the right leg was imprinted. Apologists have imagined that the leg was outstretched but the lower end of the cloth was turned up to cover the feet; yet to remain in place, the end of the cloth would almost surely have to be folded well over the top of the foot, leading to the added imprint of the top of the foot and toes. In addition, the front image would be abruptly terminated by this flap of cloth.

Other details are suggestive. If we accept the view of most authenticity advocates that the position of the feet implies that they were nailed together rather than separately, we must also recognize that this was a European artistic concept that had become conventional by the time the shroud first appeared. Also, the shroud depicts the lance wound in Jesus' right side, where artists have invariably placed it; however, only the Gospel of John mentions this wound and does not specify which side was pierced (Nickell 1998, 57–75).

Among realistic details that are supposed to be beyond the knowledge of a medieval artist are flagellation marks on the body image. However, medical paintings depict contemporary flagellations and even show the Roman *flagrum*. Another such detail concerns nail wounds located in the wrists rather than the hands. Actually, however, only one such wound shows, and it is clearly located at the base of the palm.

Contradicting the views of shroud advocates is the opinion of one of the United States' most distinguished medical-legal experts, Dr. Michael M. Baden. Baden chaired the forensic pathology panel of the U.S. Congress Select Committee on the murders of President John F. Kennedy and Dr. Martin Luther King Jr. and served on the critical review panel for my book *Inquest on the Shroud of Turin* (1998). Baden stated, "If I had to go into a courtroom, I could not say there was rigor, whether the man was alive or dead, or that this picture was a true reflection of injuries. In no way do I hold myself out as an expert on the shroud, but I do know dead bodies. Human beings don't produce this kind of pattern" (quoted in Rhein 1980, 50). It was Baden's opinion that the shroud never held a body.

A Work of Art

The 1978 examination of the shroud by STURP, a group of mostly religious, pro-shroud scientists, included taking samples from the surface of the cloth. Clear tape was applied to lift off surface debris, which was then affixed to microscope slides. Thirty-two image, "blood," and off-image areas were sampled.

These tape samples were given to famed Chicago microanalyst Walter C. McCrone, who had been employed by art galleries world-wide to authenticate artworks. His most celebrated case involved the infamous "Vinland Map," supposedly a fifteenth-century work but actually drawn—McCrone discovered—with an ink containing anatase, a pigment not synthesized until the twentieth century. As with the shroud, McCrone's work was challenged, but he was subsequently vindicated in 2002 when scientists using Raman microprobe spectroscopy confirmed the presence of anatase (Brown and Clark 2002). McCrone's most lasting contribution to microscopy may be his multivolume work *The Particle Atlas,* a compilation of photomicrographs of various substances to aid identification. Regarded widely as one of the best forensic microscopists in the world, McCrone had at his command the most fully equipped laboratory of its type. His motto, ironic for a giant in his field, was "think small."

McCrone set to work examining the thirty-two tape samples with a polarized-light microscope. In addition to linen fibers and specks of debris, he observed traces of a fine red iron oxide, identical in appearance and properties to an iron earth pigment known as red ocher. Conducting a "blind" study (so that he did not know where on the shroud a given sample had been taken), he discovered significant amounts of the pigment on the image but not on the background. He first thought that this pigment had been applied as a dry powder but later concluded that it was a component of dilute tempera paint. The "blood" consisted of red ocher and vermilion with traces of rose madder—pigments used by medieval artists to depict blood.

STURP held McCrone to a secrecy agreement, and statements made to the press indicated that no evidence of artistry had been found. McCrone was subsequently drummed out of STURP, and its representatives paid a surprise visit to McCrone's lab to confiscate his samples (Nickell 2004a, 194).

In 1996 McCrone finally published the full story of his lengthy involvement with the shroud. Titled *Judgment Day for the Turin "Shroud,"* it is the definitive account of the scientific detection of artistic materials to uncover one of history's great forgeries. McCrone equated his findings of dilute collagen tempera with the medieval grisaille technique, a method of monochromatic painting on cloth that used transparent watercolors for the tones and left the cloth bare for the light areas. He concluded that the shroud's photonegative properties are merely due to the artist's wishing to create the effect of a bodily imprint on the cloth. McCrone bolstered his evidence for a dilute tempera medium in the image areas and attempted to account for its superficial depth of penetration into the fibers. One of his suggestions is based on the chemisorption properties of the cellulose constituting the linen fibers: the paint medium would be preferentially absorbed so that, beyond a short distance, only water would penetrate to the back of the cloth, leaving no trace after it evaporated. Presumably, the "blood" penetrated because it was applied more heavily and in a less watery solution.

McCrone's evidence of artistry combines with other evidence to provide unequivocal proof that the shroud is a medieval forgery. Stylistic and iconographic elements provide corroborative evidence that the image is indeed the work of a medieval artisan. By the eleventh century, artists had begun to depict the shroud as a single, double-length cloth (although, as related in John 20:5–7, actual Jewish burial practice was to use multiple cloths). And by the thirteenth century, we find ceremonial shrouds bearing full-length images of Jesus' body in death. In these, as in the Turin image, the hands are discreetly folded over the loins, an artistic motif that dates from the eleventh century. The existence of all these traditions in the shroud suggest that it is the work of an artist of the thirteenth century or later. And in fact, the long, thin figure is indicative of French Gothic art of the fourteenth century. When we consider the cloth's incompatibility with Jewish burial practices, the lack of provenance for thirteen centuries, the reported forger's confession, and the radiocarbon date, we have a complete scientific and scholarly case against authenticity.

The approaches of real science and "shroud science" are virtually mirror images of each other. Shroudologists have consistently begun with the desired answer and worked backward to the evidence. Lacking any viable hypothesis for the image formation, they offered one explanation for the lack of provenance (the cloth might have been hidden away), another for the forger's confession (the reporting bishop could have been mistaken), still another for the pigments (an artist copying the image could have splashed some on the cloth), and so forth.

In contrast, independent investigators allowed the preponderance of prima facie evidence to lead them to the following conclusion: the "shroud" never held a body, and its image is the handiwork of a clever medieval artisan. The evidence is appropriately corroborated as well. For example, the confession is supported by the lack of a prior record, the red "blood" and the presence of pigments are consistent with artistry, and the carbon dating is consistent with the time frame indicated by the iconographic evidence. Indeed, skeptics had predicted the results of the carbon dating virtually to the year—a measure of the accuracy of both the collective evidence and the radiocarbon testing technique.

Thus far, however, "shroud science" seems to be mounting an effective propaganda campaign. It has been well served by shroud journalism, whereby reporters' questions about authenticity are directed primarily to shroud proponents—rather like asking members of the Flat Earth Society about the curvature of the earth. Perhaps the word used most often during shroud media blitzes is "mystery." But honest journalists do not engage in mystery mongering. Instead, like all true investigators, they believe that mysteries are meant to be carefully and fairly examined. It is unfortunate that we must now recall the words of Canon Ulysse Chevalier, the Catholic historian who brought to light the documentary evidence of the shroud's medieval origin. As he lamented, "The history of the shroud constitutes a protracted violation of the two virtues so often commended by our holy books: justice and truth" (quoted in Nickell 1998, 21).

CHAPTER 10

The Sudarium *of Oviedo*

Although science has established the Shroud of Turin (see chapters 8 and 9) as a fourteenth-century forgery—rendered in tempera paint by a confessed forger and radiocarbon-dated to the time of the forger's confession (Nickell 1998; McCrone 1996)—the propaganda campaign to convince the public otherwise continues. As part of the strategy, some shroud proponents are now ballyhooing another cloth, a supposed companion burial wrapping, that they claim militates in favor of the shroud's authenticity.

Companion Relic

At issue is the Oviedo cloth, an 84- by 53-centimeter (33- by 21-inch) piece of plain-weave linen, stained with supposed blood, that some believe is the *sudarium,* or "napkin," that covered the face of Jesus in the tomb. The Gospel of John (20:7) states that it was "about his head." The cloth is kept in the Cathedral of Oviedo in an iron-grated alcove known as the *Cámara Santa* (Holy Chamber).

One reason for the interest in the Oviedo cloth among Shroud of Turin advocates is to counter the devastating radiocarbon evidence, which revealed that the shroud dated from 1260 to 1390. In response, advocates hope to link the two cloths because, allegedly, "the history of the sudarium is undisputed," and it "was a revered relic preserved from the days of the crucifixion" (Anderson 2000).

Those who hope to tie the questionable Oviedo *sudarium* to the Turin shroud—and vice versa, in the pursuit of mutual authentication—face a problem: the *sudarium* lacks an image like that on the shroud. Had such a cloth indeed covered the face of Jesus, "this would have prevented the image from being formed on the shroud, and it would presumably have caused it to be formed on the sudarium" instead (Guscin 1998, 33, 34). To solve this problem, proponents now postulate that the *sudarium* was used only temporarily, in the period after crucifixion and before burial, and that it was put aside before the body was wrapped. For some unspecified reason, "It was then placed by itself in the tomb when Jesus was buried in a shroud" (Antonacci 2000, 273). Thus it would supposedly conform to John's statement (20:7): "And the napkin, that was about his head, not lying with the linen clothes, but wrapped together in a place by itself."

However clever this rationalization, as we saw in chapter 7, John (19:40) clearly states that Jesus was buried "as the manner of the Jews is to bury," and the use of a kerchief to cover the face of the dead is specifically mentioned in the Jewish Mishnah. Also, with regard to the burial of Lazarus (John 11:44), who was "bound hand and foot with graveclothes," we are told that "his face was bound about with a napkin."

Undaunted, shroud and *sudarium* advocates have joined forces and are now making the kind of outrageous and pseudoscientific claims that used to be made for the shroud alone, declaring that "blood" and pollen evidence link the two cloths. In *The Oviedo Cloth* (see figure 10.1), Mark Guscin (1998, 110) says of the relic, "As a historical document, it confirms many of the details contained in the gospels." He adds:

> More importantly, it shows that the fourteenth century date for the Shroud obtained by the carbon dating must be mistaken. All the tests carried out on the sudarium show that it must have covered the same face as the Shroud did, and as the sudarium has been in Oviedo since 1075, the Shroud cannot possibly date from the fourteenth century. This, perhaps, is the most valuable testimony of the sudarium. All the arguments in its favour are purely scientific, not depending in any

way on faith. The investigations have had a cold, twentieth century approach, and the results point to its being genuine.

Guscin concludes:

> The tests on both the Shroud and the sudarium show that science is not opposed to faith, and in no way contradicts it. Study of the world that God made can in the end only lead us back to him. Science rather confirms faith. The words of the French priest, Roland de Vaux, although he was talking about the Dead Sea Scrolls, are also applicable to the studies on the Shroud and the sudarium, "My faith has nothing to fear from my investigations." To study Christ in a serious historical way is the duty of every Christian, and any such study can only lead to the truth about him.

But do the Oviedo cloth's supporters really rely on science, or are they following the approach of Shroud of Turin advocates, starting with the desired answer and selecting and manipulating both evidence and science until it tells them what they want to hear? As this chapter shows, the evidence allegedly supporting the cloth of Oviedo comes from some of the same dubious and discredited sources that were involved with the Turin shroud.

Historical Record

Unfortunately for the shroudologists, the historical record of the Oviedo cloth, currently located in the Cathedral of Oviedo in northern Spain, is not nearly as definitive as they imagined. First, there is not the slightest hint in the Christian Gospels or anywhere else in the New Testament that the burial wrappings of Jesus were actually preserved. Later, of course, certain apocryphal texts claimed otherwise. One fourth-century account mentioned that Peter had kept the *sudarium*, but what subsequently became of it was unknown (Wilson 1979, 92–95).

An account of the cloth was penned in the twelfth century by a bishop of Oviedo named Pelayo, who claimed that the *sudarium* had been kept in Jerusalem from the time it was discovered in the tomb until the seventh century, when Christians fleeing the Persian invasion took it to Spain. However, Pelayo is sometimes called "El Fabu-

Figure 10.1. This book—*The Oviedo Cloth* by Mark Guscin (1998)—attempts to link a Spanish linen with the Shroud of Turin. (The cover illustration is from the Book of Testaments of the Cathedral of Oviedo, which gives the history of the cloth; author's collection.)

lador" (the Storyteller) because of the untruthful details in his writings, and relic mongers typically fabricated tales about their bogus productions. Besides, there were many allegedly genuine *sudaria*, just as there were numerous "true shrouds" (Guscin 1998, 14–15).

In any case, according to Pelayo, the *sudarium* was taken to Spain in a "holy ark" made of oak and containing several other relics of the Virgin and the apostles, as well as a piece of the True Cross (Anderson 2001). Upon arriving in Spain, the refugees surrendered the ark to St. Leander, the bishop of Seville, where it was kept for several years. It was purportedly transferred to Toledo in 657, and in 718, after Muslims invaded Spain, the ark was taken for safekeeping to Oviedo. However, there are impossibilities in this tale: Leander died before the Persian invasion of Palestine occurred, and Oviedo was not founded until almost half a century after the chest was allegedly taken there (Guscin 1998, 14–15; Coulson 1958, 284). One rationalization is that the cloth was taken to a cave in the vicinity of

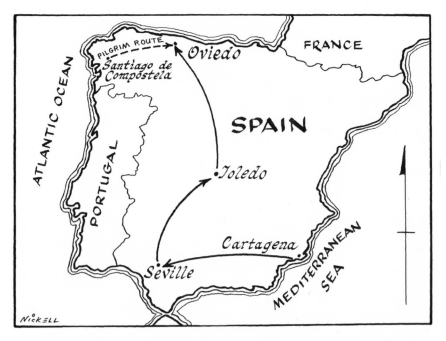

Figure 10.2. Map of Spain showing the legendary journey of the *sudarium* to Oviedo; also shown is a later pilgrims' route (drawing by author).

Oviedo. Other accounts give different versions of the cloth's Spanish travels (Guscin 1998, 14–17). (See figure 10.2.)

This is the claimed "undisputed" history that supposedly ties the cloth to the Shroud of Turin (Anderson 2000). In fact, even most pro-authenticity sources admit that it cannot be established as dating from earlier than about the eighth century (Whanger and Whanger 1998, 56), and the earliest supposed documentary evidence is from the eleventh century. According to Guscin (1998, 17), "The key date in the history of the sudarium is 14 March 1075." At that time, an oak chest in which the cloth was kept was reportedly opened by King Alfonso VI and others, including the famed knight El Cid; this is recorded in a document stating that the chest had long reposed in the church. Unfortunately, the original document has been lost, and only a thirteenth-century "copy" remains in the cathedral archives. Guscin (1998, 18) writes:

El Cid is one of the best-known characters in Spanish history. His real name was Rodrigo Díaz de Vivar, a knight in the service of Sancho and later in that of Alfonso. He was exiled by Alfonso, then reconciled with him and later exiled again. He is best remembered for conquering the Muslim kingdom of Valencia before his death in 1099. It is clear that when the ark was opened in Oviedo, he was on good terms with Alfonso. The sudarium is thus connected with one of the most popular heroes of the Middle Ages, whose deeds were celebrated in the anonymous epic poem "Cantar del Mio Cid."

The *sudarium* has remained in Oviedo in the cathedral's *Cámara Santa*. Although Oviedo was not on the famous medieval pilgrimage route to Santiago de Compostela (supposedly housing the miraculously discovered remains of Jesus' disciple James the Greater; see chapter 2), many pilgrims detoured to the Oviedo cathedral to view the *sudarium*. One modern pilgrim was the late pope John Paul II, who visited Oviedo and viewed the cloth in 1989 (Anderson 2001).

The *sudarium* is mounted in a wooden frame sheathed in silver. Handles on either side allow the frame to be held by the clergy when they use the cloth for blessings—bestowed on Good Friday and on the Feast of the Triumph of the Holy Cross. The cloth's reliquary, the wooden ark, is a chest Alfonso VI had overlaid with silver plating. On this are depicted, in relief, Christ, the four evangelists, and the twelve apostles. An inscription in Latin invites the Catholic faithful to venerate the relic containing the Holy Blood. On the silver plating is also listed the contents of the ark, including an item termed *el Santo Sudario de N.S.J.C.* (the Sacred *Sudarium* of Our Lord Jesus Christ) (Cruz 1984, 54–55; Guscin 1998, 18–20).

Bogus Science

In 1989 and 1990 a group of Turin shroud enthusiasts from the Spanish Center for Sindonology examined the *sudarium* of Oviedo. Unfortunately, their approach—based on their subsequent claims, their methodology, and the people involved—was like that used for the shroud. Their bias was evident, and the examiners appear to have decided beforehand what they would like to find and then proceeded to do so. Some of the same people whose shroud findings were disputed—by both skeptics and even strong shroud proponents—were behind the more outrageous claims regarding the *sudarium*.

The study included measuring the cloth and taking photographs, both in color and in black and white, in normal light (documenting what is visible to the naked eye) as well as ultraviolet light and infrared radiation (which could reveal latent images or other traces). The *sudarium* was also recorded on video and digitized with a program called PC-SCOPE on a personal computer. This procedure allowed the "blood" stains to be contrasted and otherwise manipulated and compared. Surface samples of dust and debris were lifted off, and minute cloth samples were also taken so that they could be studied microscopically. Reportedly, electron microscopy was employed (Guscin 1998, 21).

The only images found on the cloth were blotches and soakings of what some believe to be the "blood and water" that issued from Christ's body after it was pierced by the lance (John 19:34). Purportedly, these stains consisted of "one part blood and six parts pulmonary edema fluid" (see figure 10.3). Allegedly, "this is very significant because it helps confirm that Jesus died from asphyxiation." Presumably, a person hanging on a cross would have great difficulty breathing, causing a buildup of fluid in the lungs and its later issuance, if the body were "moved or jolted," from the nostrils (Guscin 1998, 22–25). (The "blood" on the cloth is discussed in chapter 11.)

However, "the most striking thing about all the stains is that they coincide exactly with the face on the Turin Shroud," asserts Guscin (1998, 27). He touts the initial work of a priest, Monsignor Giulio Ricci, followed by that of Dr. Alan Whanger, whom he describes as a "highly respected scientist" (32); he also praises what Whanger calls the polarized image overlay technique. Actually, Whanger is a retired geriatric psychiatrist and former missionary who took up image analysis as a hobby. He is the Shroud of Turin enthusiast mentioned in chapter 9 who perceived a hammer, a Roman thrusting spear, a pair of sandals, and other ridiculous imaginings on the shroud. More sensible shroud writers such as Ian Wilson (1998, 242) have distanced themselves from such subjective, pious illusions.

84 × 53 cm *linen cloth* *silver-sheathed wood frame* *burn hole*

stains of alleged blood & pulmonary edema fluid

The Sudarium of Oviedo

Figure 10.3. Author's sketch of the Oviedo cloth—the purported holy *sudarium* of Christ—illustrates its main features, including an apparent candle burn.

Mary Whanger explains that her husband used a superimposition technique involving polarized filters and two projectors to compare two images—such as the shroud face and Christ's face painted on an ancient icon—being "able to observe the two images fade in and out of one another" (Whanger and Whanger 1998, 17). Dr. Whanger would "first superimpose two images, using what he came to consider 'best possible alignment': eyebrows, tip of nose, and mouth." Then he and Mrs. Whanger would do comparisons, tracing "points of congruence" on clear plastic sheets (Whanger and Whanger 1998, 19).

Although overlays may be used cautiously by forensic anthropologists to compare, for example, two possible photographs of the same person, matching the shroud face with other painted or embossed faces of Jesus is pseudoscientific nonsense, and so is the Whangers' conclusion: "Our comparisons over the years of hundreds of icons with each other and with the shroud face have demonstrated that the model was the Shroud of Turin." Yet their assertion is betrayed by their waffling: "Of course, there are differences in interpretation. Some artists are more skillful than others. Also, even though there is good evidence that in early years the images on the Shroud were more apparent than they are now, still they were fragmentary, and some artists would incorporate certain features while others would choose other markings" (Whanger and Whanger 1998, 21).

The foolishness of this approach can be demonstrated by an analogous (split-image) technique that supposedly shows that "'The Mona Lisa' is Leonardo's self-portrait"—according to Picknett and Prince (1994, 130), with their customarily blithe lack of judgment. They also believe that the face on the Shroud of Turin is another Leonardo self-portrait but concede, "The fact is that there is not enough information about Leonardo's appearance to make hard-and-fast comparisons" (1994, 131).

Whanger found numerous points of correspondence between the "blood" stains on the Oviedo cloth and the image on the Shroud of Turin, concluding that the *sudarium* covered the same face as the shroud. Others are not so sure: Guscin (1998, 32) equivocates, saying, "if this is so," and lawyer Antonacci (2000, 274) shrewdly hedges his bets, claiming, "should the Oviedo Cloth be confirmed as being from around the seventh or eighth century, it would not affect the extensive evidence" in favor of the shroud.

One test of Whanger's claims is to look at the distinctive "blood" stains on the shroud's facial image and see whether they are unmistakably present on the Oviedo cloth. Perhaps the most unique stain is one on the forehead in the shape of a mirror-image "3." However, this is absent from the Oviedo cloth, a fact that Guscin (1998, 29) terms "surprising." Indeed, Guscin acknowledges one of the glaring problems faced by those who claim correspondence between the stains on the two alleged grave cloths: "Strangely enough, the area corresponding to the forehead on the sudarium is surprisingly free of blood stains, whereas the same area on the Shroud is covered with blood" (30). Undeterred in their efforts to manipulate science to support their beliefs, partisans like Guscin turn to Whanger, who is ever helpful: "He suggests that if the sudarium was used to cover Jesus' face from the foot of the cross to the tomb, the crown of thorns could have still been present on his head, restricting contact in this area." Unfortunately, there is a stain there, Guscin lamely concedes, "which must have been produced by some kind of contact" (30).

Still another purported link between the Turin and Oviedo cloths concerns pollen. As discussed in chapter 8, the shroud supposedly bears certain pollens characteristic of Palestine, Constantinople, and ancient Edessa, seemingly confirming a theory of the shroud's missing early history. Similarly, pollens supposedly discovered on the Oviedo cloth seem to confirm its purported historical route from Jerusalem through north Africa to Toledo and Oviedo; indeed, according to Guscin (1998, 22), they "perfectly match" the route. But perhaps the match is too good to be true.

The pollens on the Oviedo cloth were reported by Swiss criminologist Max Frei, the same person whose work regarding pollens on the shroud was severely criticized—even by the Shroud of Turin Research Project (Wilson 1998, 98–101; see chapter 8). It is important to note that pollen is typically identified only to the level of family or possibly genus—rarely to species. Yet of the fifty-eight pollens that Frei allegedly identified on the shroud, fifty-six were to species. Smithsonian botanist Richard H. Eyde and others expressed concerns about these claims (Nickell 1994, 381–82; Wilson 1998, 103), even before microanalyst Walter McCrone reviewed Frei's samples and suggested possible skullduggery (Nickell 1994, 384).

When we turn to the alleged pollens on the Oviedo cloth, the same concerns apply. Frei reportedly claimed that he could identify pollens from the route the cloth legendarily took: from Jerusalem to north Africa, Toledo, and finally Oviedo. Guscin (1998, 22) also noted, "There was nothing relating the sudarium to Constantinople, France, Italy or any other country in Europe." This evidence is doubtful if not outright preposterous. Unless new samples are taken from the Oviedo cloth by expert, independent authorities, such claims should be regarded as suspect at best and bogus at worst.

Carbon Dating

The Oviedo cloth has reportedly been dated by two laboratories—to the seventh and eighth centuries, respectively—but the circumstances are confusing and controversial. The significance of such results to *sudarium* partisans can be seen in this response from Guscin (1998, 87–88):

> Carbon dating has given the following results—1260–1390! for the Shroud, and the latter half of the first millennium for the sudarium. The simple conclusion for those who refuse to accept that either cloth is genuine is that carbon dating has given correct results and those who believe in the Shroud's or the sudarium's authenticity are just religious maniacs desperately looking for proof of something that never happened. The truth, however, is that the two carbon dating results mutually annul each other. Having proved the relationship between the two cloths, if one dating is correct, the other must be incorrect, and if one of them is incorrect the other one can be too. Carbon dating does not stand up to the test of any other scientific investigation.

Actually, the only "relationship between the two cloths" seems to be that both are medieval fakes. When done properly, as it was with the Shroud of Turin, radiocarbon dating is an excellent investigative technique. But was it done properly in the case of the *sudarium* of Oviedo?

Reportedly, there were two radiocarbon analyses performed on Oviedo cloth samples, yielding dates of circa a.d. 679 and circa a.d. 710 (Antonacci 2000, 273)—a rather close agreement. Unfortunately, there were irregularities—questions of competence and possible deceptive practices—in the submission of the samples. Apparently, samples from the Oviedo cloth were taken by Monsignor Giulio Ricci, a lifelong shroud zealot, some fifteen years before the carbon dating was performed. They were sent with insufficient documentation, and one sample was—for whatever reason—misstated by the sender to be from the eleventh century. Reportedly, the samples were not submitted as swatches but had already been combusted (a stage required in the dating process) and were supposedly received at the

University of Arizona as ampoules of carbon dioxide gas that had, unfortunately, leaked air. There is some question whether this rendered the samples unusable, and therefore the dating was not carried out, or whether the tests were done but were of doubtful reliability (Guscin, 1998, 77–84).

Other tests were done using a sample sent by Pierluigi Baima-Bollone. A letter dated October 31, 1990, and signed by Jodi Barnhill of the University of Arizona reported (according to Guscin 1998, 82) a calendar age of a.d. 642 to 869, with a 95 percent confidence level (or a.d. 666 to 771—a narrower range—but at a confidence level of only 68 percent). Another sample, reportedly sent by Mario Moroni, was also carbon-dated, according to a letter dated September 6, 1992, and signed by A. J. T. Jull of the University of Arizona. That sample, which was apparently falsely labeled "linen cloth, Copta [*sic*] tomb," was determined to date from a.d. 540 to 754, with a 95 percent confidence level (or a.d. 598 to 666 at 68 percent confidence) (Guscin 1998, 82–83). Regarding the issue of questionable labeling, Jull observed (quoted in Guscin 1998, 83):

> The second [sample] was stated . . . to be a sample of 11th century linen. The second sample was also used by Mr. Moroni in some heating experiments, which suggests they were not particularly valuable. Unfortunately, no detailed provenance information was provided by Moroni or his colleagues. In order to produce a radiocarbon date on any particular material, it is important that the origin of the samples be known and clearly stated to the laboratory. In the case of samples of particular archaeological interest, it is important to follow the correct protocols in order that samples ages are not represented as something else at a later date. I do not think this has happened here.

If the tests were properly done on samples taken from the Oviedo cloth—an uncertainty, at this point—the cloth appears to date from circa 695, not long before the cloth was reportedly taken to Oviedo in 718.

Already, *sudarium* propagandists are trying to find ways to circumvent the reported carbon-14 dating. According to *Crisis* magazine, "those who contend it is older say the test results were distorted by the effects of a terrorist bombing inside the cathedral in 1934" (Anderson 2001, 41). That is a ludicrous apologetic, but it may well be sufficient for those who are determined to believe, no matter what.

CHAPTER 11

Blood of Jesus

Although the central symbol of Christianity is the cross, a piece of Jesus' cross would only be a second-class relic (one that touched his body; see chapter 1), whereas a trace of his blood would represent a first-class relic (an actual part of his body). If genuine, it would constitute evidence of Jesus' historical existence, as well as provide a powerful reminder of his Crucifixion and death. Here, I examine the various alleged traces of Jesus' blood, especially those on the Shroud of Turin and the *sudarium* of Oviedo.

Holy Blood

In his *Treatise on Relics*, John Calvin (1543, 49–50, 56) decried relic mongering in general, saying, "the desire for relics is never without superstition, and what is worse, it is usually the parent of idolatry." He also enumerated many instances of specific abuse:

> Let us begin with Jesus Christ, about whose blood there have been fierce disputations; for many maintained that he had no blood except of a miraculous kind; nevertheless the natural blood is exhibited in more than a hundred places. They show at Rochelle a few drops of it, which, as they say, was collected by Nicodemus in his glove. In some places they have phials full of it, as, for instance at Mantua and elsewhere; in other parts they have cups filled with it, as in the Church of St. Eustache at Rome.
> They did not rest satisfied with simple blood; it was considered

necessary to have it mixed with water as it flowed out of his side
when pierced on the cross [John 19:34]. This is preserved in the
Church of St. John of the Lateran at Rome.

Calvin continued:

> Now, I appeal to the judgment of every one whether it is not an evident
> lie to maintain that the blood of Jesus Christ was found, after a lapse of
> seven or eight hundred years, to be distributed over the whole world,
> especially as the ancient church makes no mention of it?

Acknowledging that several places claimed to have relics of the
"Precious Blood" (in its entry of that title), the *Catholic Encyclopedia* (1913) observes that such claims were made "on the strength of
ancient traditions." However, it acknowledges that "it is often difficult to tell whether the traditions are correct."

Something of the dubiety of such a blood relic, as well as the
veneration accorded it, is seen in the "relic of the Precious Blood"
kept in the church at Weingarten, Germany (near Ravensburg). According to the *Catholic Encyclopedia* (1913, s.v. "Weingarten"):

> Its legend runs thus: Longinus, the soldier who opened the Savior's
> side with a lance, caught some of the Sacred Blood and preserved it in
> a leaden box, which later he buried at Mantua. Being miraculously
> discovered in 804, the relic was solemnly exalted by Leo III, but again
> buried during the Hungarian and Norman invasions. In 1048 it was re-
> discovered and solemnly exalted by Pope Leo IX in the presence of the
> emperor, Henry III, and many other dignitaries. It was divided into
> three parts, one of which the pope took to Rome, the other was given
> to the emperor, Henry III, and the third remained at Mantua. Henry III
> bequeathed his share of the relic to Count Baldwin V of Flanders, who
> gave it to his daughter Juditha. After her marriage to Guelph IV of
> Bavaria, Juditha presented the relic to Weingarten.

That occurred in 1090 in a solemn procession. The Precious Blood
was kept at a Benedictine monastery until the abbey was suppressed
in 1802. (Later it became an infantry barracks.) The reliquary is kept
in the abbey church in Weingarten. It is only a gilded copper replica,
since the original—of solid gold, set with jewels—was confiscated by
the government when the monastery was suppressed.

Another alleged specimen of Christ's blood is the relic of the Holy Blood at Bruges, Belgium, a famous pilgrimage center. According to a pious legend, the relic was obtained in Palestine by Thierry of Alsace during the Second Crusade in the mid-twelfth century. Reportedly, his relative Baldwin III, who was king of Jerusalem, presented it to him as a reward for meritorious service, although "the chronicles of the crusades never mention the presence of the relic in Jerusalem" (Aspesiag 1988, 10). Thierry supposedly brought the relic to Bruges in 1150; however, another source says that it arrived in 1204, and the earliest document referring to it is dated 1270 (*Catholic Encyclopedia* 1913, s.v. "Bruges"; Aspesiag 1988, 9–11). In 1303 a solemn Procession of the Holy Blood was instituted to commemorate the city's deliverance from French tyranny the previous May. To this day, it remains "one of the great religious celebrations in Belgium, to which thousands congregate from all parts" (*Catholic Encyclopedia* 1913, s.v. "Bruges").

A less solemn exposition occurs daily for the veneration of the faithful. I visited the Basilica of the Holy Blood in Bruges (see figure 11.1) on October 25, 2006, and held in my hands the reliquary supposedly containing Christ's blood. I also obtained useful texts (e.g., Aspesiag 1988). The "clotted blood" is kept in what has been determined to be a Byzantine perfume bottle of the eleventh or twelfth century. The bottle is of rock crystal rather than glass; its neck is wound with gold thread, and its stopper is sealed with red wax. It is set in a glass-fronted cylinder covered at each end with golden coronets decorated with angels (see figure 11.2). On the frame is "MCCCLXXXVIII die III maii" (May 3, 1388). There is no proof that the "blood" is genuine; the "coagulated drops" appear suspiciously red (see color photograph in *Bruges Tourist Guide* 1998, 28). A papal bull issued in 1310 by Pope Clement V granted indulgences to pilgrims who visited the chapel and worshipped the blood, which was said to return to its original liquid state each Friday at noon. (This evokes the "miracle" of the blood of St. Januarius of Naples, discussed in chapter 2.) Supposedly, as a result of some blasphemy that occurred later that year, the miracle ceased, occurring only one more time, in 1388 (Aspesiag 1988, 11). At best, it was a temporary miracle; more likely, it was a pious fraud.

I had better luck witnessing a relic of the Holy Blood in Turin, Italy, kept in the Church of Maria Ausiliatrice. The church's crypt contains a fabulous collection of some five thousand relics of saints, exhibited in seemingly endless panels and display cases along the walls. The chapel is also celebrated for its connection to St. Giovanni Don Bosco (1815–1888), an Italian priest who founded the order of Salesian Fathers. A brass cross in the floor of the chapel supposedly marks the spot where the Virgin Mary appeared to him and told him that she wanted a church built there—the site of the martyrdom, in about A.D. 300, of three Roman legionnaires. The focal point of the chapel is a lighted cross containing, purportedly, a piece of the True Cross and a small amount of the Holy Blood of Christ (see figure 11.3). As with other such blood relics, there is no credible evidence to link it with Jesus or even with his time.

In *Treatise on Relics*, Calvin (1543, 71–72) comments on "the miraculous blood which has flowed from several hosts [communion wafers],—as, for instance, in the Churches of St. Jean-en-Grève at Paris, at St. Jean d'Angeli at Dijon, and in many other places. They show even the penknife with which the host at Paris was pierced by a Jew, and which the poor Parisians hold in as much reverence as the host itself." Joan Carroll Cruz (1984, 10) also discussed several of these "eucharistic miracles," among them one mentioned by St. Cyprian in the third century.

The most publicized such "miracle" was reported in the eighth century at Lanciano, Italy. A monk celebrating Mass supposedly had doubts about transubstantiation—the Roman Catholic belief that communion bread and wine literally become the body and blood of Christ when consecrated by an ordained priest. Suddenly, the Host was transformed into a disc of flesh, and the wine turned into blood. The blood in the chalice was further transformed into five pellets of various shapes and sizes; yet it was claimed that one pellet weighed

(Right) Figure 11.1. The Basilica of the Holy Blood in Bruges, Belgium, has an alleged blood relic of Christ (photo by author).

(Below) Figure 11.2. Painting in the basilica at Bruges depicts the stoppered bottle with the reputed Holy Blood, contained in a glass cylinder with golden coronets (photo by author).

WAERAGTIGE AFBEELDINGE
VAN HET HEYLIG BLOED
ONS HEEREN JESU CHRISTI

Figure 11.3. This lighted cross in the relic chapel of
the Church of Maria Ausiliatrice in Turin displays a
purported relic of the Holy Blood, as well as an
alleged piece of the True Cross (photo by author).

as much as all five, two were as heavy as any three, and the smallest
pellet weighed as much as the largest one (Cruz 1984, 10–11). The
flesh and blood pellets were housed in a reliquary, and in the sixteenth century, the prodigy of the weighing was repeated. However,
it has subsequently failed, including the most recent examination in
1970. Odoardo Linoli, a professor of anatomy and histology, examined the relics and reported that the flesh was muscular tissue of the

heart wall and that both it and the pellets were type AB blood. He asserted that fraud was conclusively eliminated, but his reasons were dubious: he claimed that the blood would have spoiled and that the flesh would have to have been cut by an expert (Cruz 1984, 11–13). These opinions, however, seem subjective and overstated.

Indeed, the Lanciano "miracle" sounds like a staged event, designed to show the triumph of a controversial belief by having God perform the equivalent of a magic trick. The characterization of the unnamed monk as having doubts—as being "versed in the sciences of the world, but ignorant in that of God" (Cruz 1984, 10, quoting an "ancient document")—seems intended to portray him as a doubting Thomas type. Making a believer of a skeptic is the fervent wish of everyone who engages in superstitious thinking. The "miracle" is supposed to render the event in question completely convincing—even to a skeptic.

Another example shows how these eucharistic miracle tales are intended to provide proof of the truth of transubstantiation. As Cruz (1984, 14–15) summarizes the story:

> The miracle originated in the parish of St. Stephen, located in Santarem, Portugal, 35 miles south of Fatima. A woman of the parish, unhappy with the activities of an unfaithful husband, had consulted a sorceress who promised a deliverance from her trials for the price of a consecrated host. After many hesitations the woman consented, received Holy Communion, but removed the Host from her mouth and wrapped it in her veil with the intention of conveying it to the sorceress. Within moments blood issued from the Host and increased in volume until it dripped from the cloth, thereby attracting the attention of bystanders. On seeing blood on the woman's hand and arm, and thinking her injured, the witnesses rushed forward to help. The woman avoided their concern and ran to her home, leaving a trail of blood behind her. Hoping to hide the bloody veil and its contents, she placed them in a chest; but during the night she was obliged to reveal her sin to her husband when a mysterious light penetrated the trunk and illuminated the house.

Cruz continues:

> Both knelt in adoration for the remaining hours until dawn, when the priest was summoned. News of the mysterious happenings spread

quickly, attracting countless people who wished to contemplate the miracle. Because of the furor, an Episcopal investigation was promptly initiated.

The Host was soon taken in procession to the Church of St. Stephen where it was encased in wax and secured in the tabernacle. Sometime later, when the tabernacle was opened, another miracle was discovered. The wax that had encased the Host was found broken in pieces with the Host now enclosed in a crystal pyx. The Host was later placed in the gold and silver monstrance in which it is still contained.

This story is as implausible as it is obviously propagandistic. It may have been effective for the credulous thirteenth-century faithful, but not, one hopes, for today's rational thinkers. The same may be said of the many other eucharistic miracle tales.

"Blood" on the Shroud

At first look, the "blood" on the Shroud of Turin—the alleged Holy Blood from Jesus' Crucifixion—appears highly suspect (except to shroud zealots). The stains are still bright red ("carmine" is a frequent description), unlike genuine blood, which quickly turns brown and eventually blackens with age (Kirk 1974, 194–95). These color transitions are so characteristic of aging blood that forensic scientists have employed spectrophotometric data to assist them in estimating the age of bloodstains (Nickell 1998, 128).

The stains are also unnaturally picturelike, flowing in neat artistic rivulets. For example, "blood" from the "scalp wounds" trickles on the outside of the locks. However, as pathologist Michael Baden observed, "When the scalp bleeds, it doesn't flow in rivulets; the blood mats on the hair." He added, "To me, this makes the image less real. It's all too good to be true. I'd expect to see a pool of blood. Whatever did this doesn't speak for severe scalp lacerations" (quoted in Rhein 1980, 50).

Moreover, how could some of the "clots" or flows of dried blood (as on the arms) have transferred to the cloth at all? And how could wet blood, which supposedly flowed onto the cloth after the body was wrapped in it, have dried without adhering to the cloth? And if such blood had not dried, how could it have remained undisturbed when the cloth was removed from the body?

As mentioned in chapter 8, the secret commission created to study the Shroud of Turin (1969–1976) included internationally known forensic serologists—blood experts—who made heroic efforts to validate the "blood." Yet all the microscopic, chemical, biological, and instrumental tests were negative. The experts discovered reddish granules that would not dissolve in reagents that dissolve blood, and one investigator found traces of what appeared to be paint (Nickell 1998, 128–29). Subsequently, as discussed in chapter 9, the distinguished microanalyst Walter McCrone found that the "blood" actually consisted of red ocher and vermilion pigments, along with traces of rose madder, in a collagen tempera binder. These pigments were used by medieval artists to depict blood in their paintings.

McCrone's samples were given to two late additions to the Shroud of Turin Research Project (STURP), John Heller and Alan Adler, neither of whom was a forensic serologist or a pigment expert. Indeed, Heller admitted that McCrone "had over two decades of experience with this kind of problem and a worldwide reputation," whereas Heller conceded that he and Adler "had never before tackled anything like an artistic forgery" (Heller 1983, 168). That being the case, one wonders why they were chosen for such important work.

Heller and Adler soon proclaimed that they had identified the presence of blood on the shroud samples. However, at the 1983 conference of the prestigious International Association for Identification, forensic analyst John F. Fischer explained how results similar to theirs could have been obtained from tempera paint. They had used a forensically invalid method to identify blood—a this-plus-this approach. But blood is not identified by adding positive results for the presence of iron, protein, and the like, especially since a red ocher (iron oxide) tempera paint would also test positive for these substances. Crucially, not a single test conducted by Heller and Adler was specific for blood, in contrast to the tests conducted by the secret commission's forensic serologists, which yielded consistently negative results (Fischer 1983).

Heller and Adler did find considerable amounts of ferric oxide and a single particle of vermilion; the latter supported McCrone's findings, although not in the quantity he found. The lesser amount of vermilion may be attributable to McCrone's sophisticated instrumentation, which was much more capable of detecting the vermilion particles (among the similarly birefringent iron oxide ones) than was conventional microscopic examination, as McCrone himself discovered.

Another claim regarding the "blood" was made by a zealous shroud partisan and chairman of a shroud center, Dr. Pierluigi Baima-Bollone, a professor of legal medicine. He reported that the "blood" on the shroud was real and even identified it as type AB—a finding utterly negated by the tests of the forensic serologists on the secret commission. Even though the "blood" had failed their preliminary tests for blood, they still attempted to type and speciate the red substance, without success.

Ian Wilson, one of the shroud's most committed defenders, barely mentions Bollone's alleged blood typing, merely remarking in *The Blood and the Shroud* (1998, 89) that Bollone "claimed to" have made such a determination. And STURP's Ray Rogers (2004) commented that although he believed the blood was real, "the things you hear about typing are nonsense." Put another way, Bollone's claims are baloney.

Another remarkable claim is that a University of Texas scientist discovered a trace of human DNA on a sample taken from a shroud bloodstain. Aside from questions about the specimen's authenticity, the scientist, Victor Tryon, never claimed that the blood on the cloth was real. Tryon told *Time* magazine, "All I can tell you is that DNA contamination is present and that the DNA belonged either to a human or another higher primate. I have no idea who or where the DNA signal came from, nor how long it's been there." He never said that the DNA came from blood. As he observed, "Everyone who has ever touched the shroud or cried over the shroud has left a potential DNA signal there" (Van Biema 1998, 61). Soon after he conducted the tests, Tryon quit the group he was working with, saying, "I saw it as a multidisciplinary project involving archaeology, physiology, and other fields. But I came to believe there was another agenda present, too. It was my first encounter with zealotry in science."

"Blood" on the Sudarium

The cloth of Oviedo—the alleged *sudarium* that many believe was a "companion cloth" to the Shroud of Turin—also purportedly bears the blood of Jesus, as discussed in chapter 10. Mark Guscin (1998, 22) asserts that "the main stains consist of one part blood and six parts pulmonary oedema fluid." He does not explain how this was determined or why it might not be blood to which water was added. In addition, one must keep in mind that the stains on the Oviedo cloth could consist of genuine blood, even human blood, yet still be the seventh-century fake that other evidence suggests it is.

At an international congress in Oviedo in October 1994, papers were presented focusing on the latest investigations of the supposed *sudarium*. Supposedly it was established that the "bloodstains" on the cloth were not only human blood but were also type AB—"the same group as the blood on the shroud" (Guscin 1998, 56). According to a writer for *Crisis* magazine, "This was a crucial test, for had the blood types not matched, any subsequent testing would be pointless" (Anderson 2001, 39). Guscin (1998, 56) acknowledges that the matching of the blood types "could be described as coincidence, but," he adds, "taken in context with the rest of the studies it confirms the relationship between the two cloths."

Unfortunately, the blood typing was conducted by the same Dr. Pierluigi Baima-Bollone who claimed to have identified type AB blood on the shroud—thus accomplishing what even expert forensic serologists could not. Obviously, we must be suspicious of his assertion that there is human blood of the group AB on the Oviedo *sudarium* as well. Operating even further beyond his field of expertise, Bollone "has also studied the fabric of the sudarium, and affirmed that it is typical of the first century" (according to Guscin 1998, 56) —never mind seeking the opinion of textile experts. Bollone may be smarting over the fact that many doubt his blood typing claims (I, for example, like to joke about "type AB tempera paint"). According to one journalist (Regolo 1995), Bollone hoped that DNA analysis would yield further parallels between the two sets of stains. Samples were sent to the Institute of Legal Medicine in Genoa, which is headed by Professor Marcello Canale. Apparently, however, the shroud sample did not even come from one of the "blood" areas, and the results represented something of a fiasco for Bollone. As Canale reported (quoted in Regolo 1995):

> We received two extremely thin 1.5 cm length threads derived from the edges of the cloth, approximately from the region of the man of the Shroud's feet. We have extracted the DNA present on these tiny threads, and have amplified this with a chain reaction that allows us, via a particular enzyme, to keep on replicating the DNA an infinite number of times. It is a method that can be used even in the case of a single cell. . . . The DNA chain is very long, and we are able to identify very small sectors representing the individual from whom they derive. With regard to sexual characteristics, we have positive indications for both genders, but much more positive for the masculine one. . . . It would seem that there has been some form of contamination, as we cannot suppose that the individual represented on the stains belonged to both sexes.

The hilarity of the situation continued when DNA with both male and female characteristics was also discovered on the Oviedo cloth, leading some to hypothesize that Jesus might have been endowed with both characteristics. Canale responded (quoted in Regolo 1995): "Questions such as these are beyond our competence. But science might well explain such contamination as due to both cloths having been woven by women, also to women playing a part in the vicissitudes both underwent in the course of their history." He added, "the slightest thing, a single cell, a little skin, perspiration itself, these contaminations . . . can give a distorted result."

Such embarrassments aside, zealots like Bollone are at pains to link the *sudarium* with the shroud in the hope of boosting the credibility of the latter. One enthusiast, Mary Jo Anderson (2001, 37), suggested that the *sudarium* "may be the key to unveiling the mystery of the Shroud of Turin." The true mystery of the shroud—and of the *sudarium* as well—is why people persist in attempting to convert medieval forgeries into sacred relics. But perhaps this is not so mysterious after all. When Anderson (2001, 37) suggests that "the history and scientific findings respecting the Sudarium . . . provide an unfolding story that rivals the most pious fiction," one is tempted to point out that much of the "history" and "science" regarding the cloth *are* pious fiction. For instance, consider one early account, dating from the time of Alfonso III, in A.D. 1030. The story tells how some hapless priests, who had failed to either fast or pray, opened the wooden reliquary in the *Cámara Santa*, whereupon they were struck blind by the holy light that emanated from the ark. Anderson (2001, 38) concedes, "This account is dismissed by historians as legend." But did such a legend just originate somehow, or did someone make it up?

As to the "science" applied to the *sudarium*, why is it that only Shroud of Turin loyalists and other religious partisans are allowed full access to the cloth, rather than independent scientific and technical experts? Why are amateur hobbyists like Alan Whanger (a former psychiatrist and missionary) conducting image analyses? Why is their doubtful work being promoted by religious writers who imply that the *sudarium* and the shroud are genuine? Revealingly, the first to "study" the *sudarium* was the late Monsignor Giulio Ricci, then president of the Roman Center for Sindology. When he first viewed the cloth, he exclaimed, "It's authentic," and promptly decided that it was a companion relic to the Shroud of Turin (Anderson 2001, 39).

I recall, many years ago, encountering a devout shroud believer who told me that I was missing the point. She explained that the shroud's genuineness was not important; what was important, she said, was that if people believed it to be genuine, it could help lead them to the true religion. This end-justifies-the-means attitude is, I think, all too common among relic mongers. It helps explain the initial creation of pious fakes and then the pious tales to support them; pious "science" to seemingly authenticate them; and pious articles, books, and even TV documentaries to help publicize and promote them.

CHAPTER 12

The James Ossuary

Supposedly recently discovered, the James ossuary—a limestone mortuary box that purportedly held the remains of Jesus' brother—became the subject of controversy in 2002 (see figure 12.1). It captured the attention of theologians, secular scholars, laity, and journalists around the world. Some rushed to suggest that the inscription on it is the earliest known reference to Jesus outside the Bible, providing archaeological evidence of his historical existence. "World Exclusive!" proclaimed *Biblical Archaeology Review.* "Evidence of Jesus Written in Stone," the cover continued; "Ossuary of 'James, Brother of Jesus' found in Jerusalem." Urged the contents page: "Read how this important object came to light and how scientists proved it wasn't a modern forgery." Actually, this was a rush to judgment—to say the least.

Background

The initial report in *Biblical Archaeology Review* was written by a French scholar, André Lemaire (2002), who believed that both the artifact and its inscription were authentic. Jewish burial practice included the use of such an ossuary to store bones during the period from the first century B.C. to the Roman destruction of Jerusalem in A.D. 70 (see figure 12.2). In this tradition, the corpse would first be interred in a niche in a burial cave. After about a year, when the re-

Figure 12.1. The James ossuary purportedly once held the bones of Jesus' brother (photo by author).

mains became skeletonized, the bones were gathered into a chest, usually made from a hollowed-out block of limestone fitted with a lid (Figueras 1983, 26).

Incised on one of the James ossuary's long sides is an inscription that consists of a single line of twenty small Aramaic characters. It reads (from right to left): "Ya'akov bar Yosef akhui diYeshua"—that is, "Jacob [in English, James], son of Yosef [Joseph], brother of Yeshua [Jesus]" (see figure 12.3). Based on the script, Lemaire dates the inscription to sometime between 20 B.C. and A.D. 70. And he believes that the inscription's mention of a father named Joseph plus a brother named Jesus suggests "that this is the ossuary of the James in the New Testament," which in turn "would also mean that we have here the first epigraphic mention—from about 63 C.E.—of Jesus of Nazareth" (Lemaire 2002, 33).

Lemaire believes that the inscription has a consistency and a correctness that show "it is genuinely ancient and not a fake." The

Figure 12.2. Ossuaries—like these displayed at the Royal Ontario Museum in Toronto—were used to store bones, based on a Jewish burial practice (photo by author).

box was examined by two experts from the Geological Survey of Israel at the request of *Biblical Archaeology Review*. They found that the ossuary is coated with a gray patina. "The same gray patina is found also within some of the letters," they wrote, "although the inscription was cleaned and the patina is therefore absent from several letters." They added, "The patina has a cauliflower shape known to be developed in a cave environment." The experts also reported that they saw no evidence of "the use of a modern tool or instrument" (Rosenfeld and Ilani 2002).

Unfortunately, the cleaning of the inscription—an act of either stupidity or shrewdness—is problematic. It might have removed traces of modern tooling. And when we are told that the patina is found "within some of the letters," we certainly need to know which ones, since scholars have debated whether the phrase "brother of Jesus" might be a spurious addition to an otherwise authentic inscription (Altman 2002; Shuman 2002). It is even possible for traces of

Figure 12.3. The James ossuary's inscription seems suspiciously sharp-edged for its apparent age (photo by author).

patination in an inscription to be original when the carving is not. That could happen if shallow carving were done over a deeply pitted surface—as is the case with the James ossuary. The patinated bottoms of remnant pits could thus remain inside the fresh scribings.

In any case, the patina may not be all it is claimed. According to one forgery expert, because patination is expected with age, "The production of a convincing patina has therefore been of great interest to those engaged in faking or restoration" (Jones 1990, 258). Although false patinas are most commonly applied to metalwork, stone sculptures and artifacts—including fake "prehistoric" flint implements—have been treated to create the appearance of antiquity (Jones 1990). For example, the versatile forger Alceo Dossena (1878–1937) produced convincing patinas on marble (a hard, metamorphic limestone) that gave his works "an incredible look of age" (Sox 1987, 9).

The patina traces of the James ossuary inscription were soon questioned. Responding to the claim that patina had been cleaned from the inscription, one art expert noted that genuine patina would be difficult to remove, whereas forged patina cracks off. "This appears to be what happened with the ossuary," he concluded (John Lupia quoted in Altman 2002).

Provenance

The reason for questioning the patina is that additional evidence soon raised doubts about the ossuary's authenticity. To begin with, there is the matter of its provenance, which concerns the origin or derivation of an artifact. Experts in the field of objets d'art and other rarities use the term to refer to a work's being traceable to a particular source. For example, records may show that an artifact came from a certain archaeological dig, was subsequently owned by a museum, and then was sold by the museum to a private collector.

Provenance matters more with a sensational artifact, and an owner's refusal or inability to explain how he or she acquired an item is suspicious—a possible indicator of forgery or theft. One of my cases, for instance, concerned a purported manuscript of Lincoln's Gettysburg Address (actually, the second sheet of what was ostensibly a two-page draft, signed by Lincoln). Suspicions were raised when it was reported that the dealer who had sold the item wanted to remain anonymous, and my subsequent ultraviolet and stereomicroscopic examination revealed that it was a forgery (Nickell 1996).

With the James ossuary, the provenance still seems to be under development. Lemaire (2002) referred to the "newly revealed ossuary," which he would only say was "now in a private collection in Israel." A sidebar stated that on a recent visit to Jerusalem, "Lemaire happened to meet a certain collector by chance; the collector mentioned that he had some objects he wanted Lemaire to see." One of the objects was the James ossuary (Feldman 2002).

The owner had pleaded with reporters not to reveal his name or address, but he was apparently uncovered by the Israeli Antiquities Authority. He is Oded Golan, a Tel Aviv engineer, entrepreneur, and collector. Golan explained that he did not wish to be identified due to concerns about privacy. "It's a character issue," he told the Associated Press; "I don't like publicity" (Laub 2002). But Golan certainly received some unwanted attention when he came under investigation by the Antiquities Authority's theft unit (Scrivener 2002). Golan claimed to have bought the ossuary in the Old City (old Jerusalem) "in the 1970s," paying a few hundred dollars to an Arab antiquities dealer he can no longer identify (Van Biema 2002; Adams 2002; Wilford 2002). He said that it was the box's engraving that interested him, yet nothing in the phrase "James, son of Joseph, brother of Jesus" ever "rang a bell" in Golan's mind (Adams 2002). Incredibly, the sensational inscription had to wait three decades before finally being appreciated by André Lemaire.

Many scholars were horrified that the ossuary had apparently been looted from its burial site—and not just because looting is illegal and immoral. When an artifact is robbed of its context, that "compromises everything," according to P. Kyle McCarter Jr., who chairs the Near Eastern studies department at Johns Hopkins University. McCarter added, "We don't know where [the box] came from, so there will always be nagging doubts. Extraordinary finds need extraordinary evidence to support them" (Van Biema 2002).

Not only the box's provenance but also its contents, which might have helped establish its origins, have reportedly been lost. "Unfortunately," states Lemaire (2002), "as is almost always the case with ossuaries that come from the antiquities market rather than from a legal excavation, it was emptied." I lamented this state of affairs to a reporter (Ryan 2002), observing that the bones could have been examined by forensic anthropologists to potentially determine the cause of death. James was reportedly thrown from the top of the temple and stoned and beaten to death (Hurley 2002), so his skeletal remains might have shown evidence of such trauma.

As it turns out, Lemaire did not mention—perhaps because he did not know—that Golan has a Tupperware container of bone fragments that he says were in the ossuary when he acquired it. One piece is as large as one-half by three inches and has raised questions about potential DNA evidence. Yet, according to *Time* magazine, Golan will not allow the fragments "to be displayed or analyzed" (Van Biema 2002).

Figure 12.4. The ossuary was featured in this elaborate temporary exhibition at the Royal Ontario Museum in Toronto (photo by author).

Further Suspicions

In addition to the questionable provenance, the exterior appearance of the ossuary raises suspicions. To view the box, which was on display at the Royal Ontario Museum (see figure 12.4), I traveled to Toronto with several of my colleagues from the Center for Inquiry, including Kevin Christopher, who has degrees in classics and linguistics. We were able to get a good look at the box, and what we observed raised some eyebrows.

First of all, I was surprised to see that the ossuary was far from being "unadorned," as Lemaire (2002, 27) had reported. His statement that "the only decoration is a line forming a frame about 0.5 inch (1.2 cm) from the outer edges" is mistaken. Significantly, on the side opposite the inscribed side are circular designs, badly worn but unmistakably present (see figure 12.5).

Ossuaries are usually decorated on only one side, presumably the one intended to face out during storage (Royal Ontario Museum

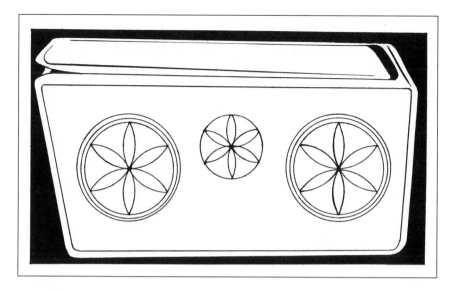

Figure 12.5. Author's drawing of the faded rosette designs on the James ossuary, located on the side opposite the inscription.

2002). If a name was added (possibly with an identifying phrase), it was apparently carved after purchase by someone such as a family member (Figueras 1983, 18). A look at a number of ossuaries shows that the name might be engraved on the decorated side if space allowed (Figueras 1983; Goodenough 1953); otherwise, it might be cut on the top, an end, or the back. Wherever it was placed, it "probably faced outwards where it could be read" (Altman 2002). In the case of the James ossuary, there would have been room on the front, yet the scribe elected to carve the inscription on the back (a possible reason for this will soon become evident).

Furthermore, the box's decorations—the carved "frame" referred to by Lemaire, which outlines all four sides, plus the circular designs —are badly worn, whereas the inscription seems almost pristine. The decorations are blurred, partially effaced, and (like much of the surface) pitted, yet the lettering is distinct and blessed with sharp edges, as if it were of recent vintage (possibly done with a dentist's drill, I quipped). My colleagues and I were all struck by that observation. So was an Israeli engineering professor, Dr. Daniel Eylon of the

University of Dayton, who noted that "sharp edges do not last 2,000 years." Eylon applied a technique used to determine whether damage to an airplane part occurred before or after an accident. Examining photographs of the inscription for scratches accrued over time, he stated, 'The inscription would be underneath these scratches if it had been on the box at the time of burial, but the majority of this inscription is on top of the scratches" (quoted in Wilford 2002).

The inscription's off-center placement in an area of the back that suffered the least time-related damage is also suspicious. Commenting on what is termed biovermiculation—that is, "limestone erosion and dissolution caused by bacteria over time in the form of pitting and etching"—one art historian stated, "The ossuary had plenty except in and around the area of the inscription. This is not normal" (Lupia quoted in Altman 2002). Indeed, that is one of the first things I observed when studying the James ossuary. It suggested to me that a forger might have selected a relatively smooth area of the back as a place to carve the small, neat characters.

Early on, the text of the inscription itself raised doubts among experts familiar with Aramaic scripts. They observed that the "James, son of Joseph" portion was in a seemingly formal script, while the "brother of Jesus" phrase was in a more cursive style. This suggested "at least the possibility of a second hand," according to one expert (McCarter quoted in Wilford 2002). Another stated, "The second part of the inscription bears the hallmarks of a fraudulent later addition and is questionable to say the least" (Rochelle Altman quoted in Wilford 2002). I felt that the perceived dichotomy in styles might simply signal that the forger was an inexpert copyist or that the effect resulted from the vagaries of stone carving.

Taken together, the various clues suggest a scenario in which a forger purchased a genuine ossuary that—lacking feet, elaborate ornamentation, or an inscription—cost little. He then obtained an Aramaic rendition of the desired wording, carved it into what seemed a good spot on the blank back, and perhaps added patination followed by "cleaning" to help explain the fresh look of the carving. Forgers frequently select genuine old artifacts on which to inflict their handiwork. Some examples that I have personally investigated and helped expose include two Daniel Boone muskets, the diary of Jack the Ripper, a *carte de visite* photo of Robert E. Lee, and a dictionary with flyleaf notes by Charles Dickens (Nickell 1990, 1996). Mounting evidence suggests that the James ossuary might be another such production.

The Verdict

I published the results of my investigation of the ossuary in *Skeptical Inquirer*, presenting evidence that an antique ossuary had been recently carved with a false inscription and possibly treated with a fake patina (Nickell 2003). That scenario was soon proved accurate by a committee of experts using a panoply of sophisticated analytical techniques.

On Wednesday, June 18, 2003, the Israeli Antiquities Authority pronounced the ossuary a fake. Officials released a statement announcing that "the inscriptions, possibly inscribed in two separate stages, are not authentic." Indeed, "the inscription appears new," the statement read, "written in modernity by someone attempting to reproduce ancient written characters." The inscription had cut through the ancient box's genuine patina, the committee of experts determined, proving that the text was a forgery (Israeli Antiquities Authority 2003). A member of the team, Uzi Dahari, stated that the inscription had recently been given a fake patina made of crushed chalk and hot water. "It's not a good fake," he concluded, decrying it as "a contamination of the archaeological science" (Nessman 2003).

In the committee's opinion, the words and phrases of the inscription had likely been found on genuine artifacts, scanned into a computer, and adjusted for size. The forger then used a program such as Adobe PhotoShop to create a realistic-appearing template. Finally, he or she incised the letters and applied the fake patina—dubbed the "James Bond"—to give the inscription the appearance of age (Maugh 2003).

The antiquities experts also branded as fake another purported archaeological treasure owned by Oded Golan, known as the "Yoash inscription." Written on a stone tablet the size of a shoebox, the inscription, supposedly dating from the ninth century B.C., was revealed in 2001. It consists of fifteen lines of ancient Hebraic writing, providing instructions for the maintenance of the Jewish Temple in Jerusalem. However, biblical language expert Avigdor Horowitz found that the inscription was rife with linguistic errors. "The person who wrote the inscription was a person who thinks in modern Hebrew," he said at a news conference. "A person thinking in biblical Hebrew would see it as ridiculous" (Israeli Antiquities Authority 2003).

In July 2003, Golan's home was raided by police, and he was arrested July 21 on suspicion of forgery of ancient artifacts. Police discovered a rooftop room that contained items in various stages of being faked with "ancient" inscriptions (Posner 2003). Also found were dental drills and tools, plus dirt from various archaeological sites that may have been used to coat fake artifacts with a layer of apparent authenticity (Samuels 2004).

Hershel Shanks—editor of *Biblical Archaeology Review*, which had touted the ossuary as genuine—was a diehard, maintaining that there had been a rush to judgment and that the evidence against the ossuary was inconclusive. His position surprised no one.

On Wednesday, December 29, 2004, Israeli prosecutors finally indicted Oded Golan and three other antiquities dealers on charges of forging the James ossuary and other biblical artifacts. Police spokesman Gil Kleiman stated, "This was a multi-million-dollar crime ring, and the suspects can expect to serve many years in prison if convicted." The indictment, running twenty-seven pages, listed eighteen counts of fraud and attempted fraud, as well as obstruction of justice (Israel 2004). Of course, Golan is presumed innocent until he is convicted in a court of law. At this writing, the preponderance of evidence indicates that *someone* forged the inscription on the James ossuary, and unless a better candidate emerges, Golan will be considered the most likely suspect.

Conclusion

As investigation after investigation has shown, not a single, reliably authenticated relic of Jesus exists. The profoundness of this lack is matched by the astonishing number of relics attributed to him. They range from his swaddling clothes and foreskin to countless artifacts of his life and Crucifixion, including his shroud—or, more appropriately, shrouds, some forty of which have been counted in Europe alone.

The Shroud of Turin has been at the center of repeated scandals, exposés, and controversies—a dubious legacy for what many consider the holiest relic in Christendom. Nevertheless, historical scholarship and scientific analyses reveal it to be a medieval fake, as is the case with so many other purported relics: the holy coat of Trier, the lance of Longinus, the Titulus, the cloth of Oviedo, the James ossuary, and on and on. The pattern is always the same: a sensational item, attended by a dubious provenance and questionable features, succumbs to impartial investigation, yet die-hard advocates continue to reject the evidence, engaging in pseudoscience—and worse—to falsely claim authenticity.

Many of today's defenders of fake relics are doubtless sincere, but they invariably begin with the desired answer and work backward to the evidence, seeking to support their prior convictions. Others, more cynical, misrepresent the evidence, believing that the end justifies the means and that the most important objective is to promote their particular religious belief. The views of Catholic scholar Canon Ulysse Chevalier—who lamented what he called "a protracted violation of the two virtues so often commended by our holy books: justice and truth"—apply to all such pious fakes. The good news is that not only secular scholars but also many Christian believers agree with Chevalier. They refuse to be taken in by fake relics and so reject the mystery mongering, pseudoscience, and outright misrepresentation involved.

That there is no authenticated physical trace of Jesus does not mean, of course, that he never existed or that he is a purely mythological figure—although it does establish the fact of the mythologizing process. Rather, it simply means that relics are not part of the evidence. The Shroud of Turin is neither Jesus' "photograph" nor proof of his resurrection. His name was not written in stone on the James ossuary; therefore, the inscription does not prove the historicity of Jesus or confirm that his father was named Joseph, as some have rushed to claim. For evidence of the historical Jesus, one must instead turn to the meager sources available—the Gospels and other Christian texts, as well as a paucity of non-Christian writings—and study their interpretations by biblical scholars.

It is an ongoing quest, and not everyone will reach the same conclusions. But at least we need not be distracted by reputed relics of the Christ that are claimed to be holy but are, in fact, the opposite.

References

Adams, Frank. 1972. *A Scientific Search for the Face of Jesus.* Tucson, Ariz.: Psychical Aid Foundation.

Adams, Paul. 2002. Ossuary's owner emerges to tell his story. *Globe and Mail* (Toronto), November 7.

Altman, Rochelle I. 2002. Final report on the James ossuary. http://web .israelinsider.com. Accessed November 6.

Anderson, Mary Jo. 2000. Scientists: Relic authenticates Shroud of Turin. *World Net Daily,* October 6. http://www.worldnetdaily.com.

———. 2001. The "other" shroud of Christ. *Crisis* (April), 36–41.

Antioch chalice. 2005. http://www.netmuseum.org/works_Of_Art/viewOne .asp?dep=7&viewmode=OEitem=50. Accessed March 16.

Antonacci, Mark. 2000. *The Resurrection of the Shroud.* New York: M. Evans and Company.

Aquinas, Thomas. 1273. *Summa Theologica,* iii, q. 25, art. 6.

Asimov, Isaac. 1969. *Asimov's Guide to the Bible.* Vol. 2, *The New Testament.* New York: Avon Books.

Aspesiag, Pierre. 1988. *Chapel of the Holy Blood, Bruges.* Ostend, Belgium: S. V. Van Mieghem A.

Attwater, Donald. 1983. *The Penguin Dictionary of Saints.* London: Penguin.

Baigent, Michael, Richard Leigh, and Henry Lincoln. 1996. *Holy Blood, Holy Grail.* London: Arrow.

Barber, Richard. 2004. *The Holy Grail: Imagination and Belief.* Cambridge, Mass.: Harvard University Press.

Barbet, Pierre. 1950. *A Doctor at Calvary,* French ed. English translation, Garden City, N.Y.: Image Books, 1963.

Bella, Francesco, and Carlo Azzi. 2002. 14C dating of the "Titulus Crucis." *Radiocarbon* 44 (3), 685–89.

Bennett, D. M. [1882]. *A Truth Seeker around the World.* New York: D. M. Bennett.

Bernstein, Amy D. 2004. Decoding the Da Vinci phenomenon. In *Secrets of the Da Vinci Code* 2004, 7–15.

Brewer, E. Cobham. 1884. *A Dictionary of Miracles.* Philadelphia: J. B. Lippincott.

Brown, Dan. 2003. *The Da Vinci Code.* New York: Doubleday.

Brown, David F. 1981. Interview with H. David Sox. *New Realities* 4, 1 (1981), 31.

Brown, Katherine L., and Robin J. H. Clark. 2002. Analysis of pigmentary materials on the Vinland Map and Tartar Relation by Raman microprobe spectroscopy. *Analytical Chemistry* 74 (15), 3658–61.

Bruges Tourist Guide. [1998]. Brussels, Belgium: Editions THILL S.A.

Burstein, Dan. 2004. The hoax behind it all. In *Secrets of the Da Vinci Code* 2004, 75.

Calvin, John. 1543. *Traité des Reliques.* Reprinted in Francis M. Higman, ed. 1970. *Jean Calvin: Three French Treatises.* London: Athlone (page numbers given are from this edition; however, quotations in English are from Krasinski 1854).

Catholic Encyclopedia. 1907–1912. New York: Robert Appleton.

Catholic Encyclopedia. 1911. Vol. 12. http://www.newadvent.org/cathen/12734a.htm. Accessed February 28, 2005.

Catholic Encyclopedia. 1913. New York: Encyclopedia Press.

Christian relics. 2004. http://www.religionfacts.com/christianity/things/relics.htm. Accessed February 28, 2005.

Coulson, John, ed. 1958. *The Saints: A Concise Biographical Dictionary.* New York: Hawthorn Books.

Cox, Simon. 2004. *Cracking the Da Vinci Code.* New York: Barnes and Noble.

Craveri, Marcello. 1967. *The Life of Jesus.* New York: Grove Press.

Cruz, Joan Carroll. 1977. *The Incorruptibles.* Rockford, Ill.: Tan Books and Publishers.

———. 1984. *Relics.* Huntington, Ind.: Our Sunday Visitor.

Damon, P. E., et al. 1989. Radiocarbon dating of the Shroud of Turin. *Nature* 337 (February 16), 611–15.

d'Arcis, Pierre. 1389. Memorandum report to Pope Clement VII. In the Collection de Champagne, Bibliothèque Nationale (Paris), vol. 154, folio 138. English translation by Herbert Thurston.

Davidson, J. Leroy, and Philippa Gerry, eds. 1939. *The New Standard Encyclopedia of Art.* New York: Garden City Publishing Co.

Duchane, Sangeet. 2004. *The Little Book of the Holy Grail.* New York: Barnes and Noble.

Dummelow, J. R., ed. 1951. *A Commentary on the Holy Bible by Various Writers.* New York: Macmillan.

Dunn, Charles W., ed. 1952. *A Chaucer Reader*. New York: Harcourt, Brace and World.

Emmerich, Anne Catherine. 1904. *The Dolorous Passion of Our Lord Jesus Christ*. Transcribed and edited by Klemens Maria Brentano, translated from the German, 20th ed. El Sobrante, Calif.: North Bay Books.

Encyclopaedia Britannica. 1960. Chicago: Encyclopaedia Britannica.

Encyclopaedia Britannica. 1978. Chicago: Encyclopaedia Britannica.

Falconi, Marta. 2005. "Trial" aims to debunk "Da Vinci Code" (Associated Press). *Buffalo News*, February 19.

Feldman, Steven. 2002. The right man for the inscription [sidebar to Lemaire]. *Biblical Archaeology Review* 29, 6 (November–December), 30.

Figueras, Pau. 1983. *Decorated Jewish Ossuaries*. Leiden, Netherlands: E. J. Brill.

Fischer, John F. 1983. A summary critique of analyses of the "blood" on the Turin "shroud." In Nickell 1998, 155–58.

Ford, David Nash. 2005. The Marian chalice. http://www.earlybritish kingdoms.com/arthur/marian.html. Accessed March 17.

Garlaschelli, Luigi. 2004. Personal communications, October 15–16, and typescript, Miraculous Italian blood relics, n.d.

Garlaschelli, Luigi, et al. 1991. Letter to *Nature* 353 (October 10), 507.

Garza-Valdez, Leoncio. 1999. *The DNA of God?* New York: Doubleday.

Geberth, Vernon J. 1993. *Practical Homicide Investigation*. Boca Raton, Fla.: CRC Press.

Gies, Frances, and Joseph Gies. 1990. *Daily Life in Medieval Times*. New York: Barnes and Noble Books.

Goodenough, Erwin R. 1953. *Jewish Symbols in the Greco-Roman Period*, vol. 3. New York: Pantheon Books.

Graham, Lloyd M. 1975. *Deceptions and Myths of the Bible*. Secaucus, N.J.: University Books.

Gray, Andrew. 1996. Thousands flock to view Jesus' garment. (Reuters). *Newark (N.J.), Star-Ledger*, April 20.

Guscin, Mark. 1998. *The Oviedo Cloth*. Cambridge: Lutterworth Press.

Haggard, Howard W. 1929. *Devils, Drugs and Doctors*. New York: Harper and Row.

Heller, John. 1983. *Report on the Shroud of Turin*. New York: Houghton Mifflin.

Humber, Thomas. 1978. *The Sacred Shroud*. New York: Pocket Books.

Hurley, Amanda Kolson. 2002. The last days of James [sidebar to Lemaire]. *Biblical Archaeology Review* 29, 6 (November–December), 32.

Hynek, R. W. 1951. *The True Likeness*. New York: Sheed and Ward.

Israel charges "Jesus box" relics ring with fraud. 2004. Reuters, December 30. http://www.reuters.com/printerFriendlyPopup.jhtml?type=World News&storyID=7201193.

Israeli Antiquities Authority says "James ossuary" inscription a fake. 2003. http://abclocal.go.com/wabc/news/print_wabc_061803_jamesbox.html. Accessed August 19.

Janson, H. W. 1963. *History of Art.* New York: Harry N. Abrams.

Jones, Alison. 1994. *The Wordsworth Dictionary of Saints.* Ware, England: Wordsworth Editions.

Jones, Mark, ed. 1990. *Fake? The Art of Deception.* Berkeley: University of California Press.

Kirk, Paul L. 1974. *Crime Investigation,* 2nd ed. New York: John Wiley and Sons.

Knuehl, Gerhard. 1996. A last relic of Christ? *Our Sunday Visitor* (August 11), 5.

Krasinski, Count Valerian. 1854. *A Treatise on Relics by John Calvin.* Newly translated from the French original, with an introductory dissertation. Edinburgh: Johnstone and Hunter. http://www.godrules.net/library/calvin/176calvin1.htm. Accessed March 28, 2005.

Larhammar, Dan. 1995. Severe flaws in scientific study criticizing evolution. *Skeptical Inquirer* 19, 2 (March–April), 30–31.

Laub, Karin. 2002. Ancient burial box isn't for sale, owner says. *Buffalo News,* November 8.

Lemaire, André. 2002. Burial box of James the brother of Jesus. *Biblical Archaeology Review* 28, 6 (November–December), 24–33, 70.

The Lost Books of the Bible and the Forgotten Books of Eden. 1976. New York: William Collins and World Publishing.

Lowenthal, David. 1998. Fabricating heritage. *History and Memory* 10, 1 (spring). http://iupjournals.org.history/ham10–1.html. Accessed March 7, 2005.

Lüdemann, Gerd. 2001. *Jesus after 2000 Years: What He Really Said and Did.* Amherst, N.Y.: Prometheus Books.

Maugh, Thomas H., II. 2003. Burial box of Jesus' brother ruled a fraud. *Los Angeles Times,* June 19.

McCrone, Walter C. 1993. Letters to the author, June 11, 30.

———. 1996. *Judgment Day for the Turin "Shroud."* Chicago: Microscope Publications.

McGuire, Tom. 1999. Is this cup the Holy Grail? *Catholic Digest* (February), 7–11.

McNeal, Edgar Holmes. 1936. *The Conquest of Constantinople.* Translated from the Old French. Columbia University Records of Civilization 23. New York: Columbia University Press.

Metzger, Bruce M., and Michael D. Coogan. 2001. *The Oxford Essential Guide to People and Places in the Bible,* American ed. New York: Berkley Books.

Meyer, Karl E. 1971. Were you there when they photographed my Lord? *Esquire* (August), 72–74, 120–24.

The Mysterious Man of the Shroud. 1997. CBS documentary, April 1.

Nessman, Ravi. 2003. James inscription called a fake (Associated Press). *Arizona Daily Star*, June 19.

New Catholic Encyclopedia. 1967. New York: McGraw-Hill.

Nickell, Joe. 1990. *Pen, Ink, and Evidence: A Study of Writing and Writing Materials for the Penman, Collector, and Document Detective.* Reprint, New Castle, Del.: Oak Knoll Press, 2000.

———. 1991. Les preuves scientifique que le Linceul de Turin date du moyen age. *Science et Vie* (July), 6–17.

———. 1993. *Looking for a Miracle: Weeping Icons, Relics, Stigmata, Visions and Healing Cures.* Buffalo, N.Y.: Prometheus Books.

———. 1994. Pollens on the "shroud": A study in deception. *Skeptical Inquirer* 18, 4 (summer), 379–85.

———. 1996. *Detecting Forgery.* Lexington: University Press of Kentucky.

———. 1998. *Inquest on the Shroud of Turin.* Amherst, N.Y.: Prometheus Books.

———. 2001. *Real-Life X-Files.* Lexington: University Press of Kentucky.

———. 2003. Bone (box) of contention. *Skeptical Inquirer* 27, 2 (March–April), 19–22.

———. 2004a. *The Mystery Chronicles: More Real-Life X-Files.* Lexington: University Press of Kentucky.

———. 2004b. Relics of the Christ. Part 1 of a two-part lecture (part 2 by Gerd Lüdemann), History vs. myth. Amherst, N.Y., Center for Inquiry, July 17.

———. 2004c. "Visions" behind *The Passion. Skeptical Inquirer* 28, 3 (May–June), 11–13.

———. 2005. Claims of invalid "shroud" radiocarbon date cut from whole cloth. *Skeptical Inquirer* 29, 3 (May–June), 14–16.

Nickell, Joe, and John F. Fischer. 1992. *Mysterious Realms.* Buffalo, N.Y.: Prometheus Books.

Olson, Carl E., and Sandra Miesel. 2004. *The Da Vinci Hoax: Exposing the Errors in* The Da Vinci Code. San Francisco: Ignatius Press.

O'Neill, Brendan. 2004. The never-ending search. BBC News. http:// newsvote.bbc.co.uk/mpapps/pagetools/print/news.bbc.co.uk/2/hi/uk_ news/magazin. Accessed December 10.

Panofsky, Erwin. 1953. *Early Netherlandish Painting.* Cambridge, Mass.: Harvard University Press.

Phillips, Graham. 2004. *The Chalice of Magdalene: The Search for the Cup That Held the Blood of Christ.* Rochester, Vt.: Bear and Company.

Pick, Christopher, ed. 1979. *Mysteries of the World.* Secaucus, N.J.: Chartwell Books.

Pickett, Thomas J. 1996. Can contamination save the Shroud of Turin? *Skeptical Briefs* (June), 3.

Picknett, Lynn, and Clive Prince. 1994. *Turin Shroud: In Whose Image? The Truth behind the Centuries-Long Conspiracy of Silence.* New York: HarperCollins.

———. 1998. *The Templar Revelation.* New York: Touchstone.

Piece of the week. 2001. http://www.forbes.com/2001/01/31/0131pow .html.

Polidoro, Massimo. 2004a. What a bloody miracle! *Skeptical Inquirer* 28, 1 (January–February), 18–20.

———. 2004b. The secrets of Rennes-le-Château. *Skeptical Inquirer* 28, 6 (November–December), 22–24.

Posner, Michael. 2003. Forgery mystery creates a Pandora's box. *Globe and Mail* (Toronto), July 26.

Price, Robert M. 2003. *The Incredible Shrinking Son of Man: How Reliable Is the Gospel Tradition?* Amherst, N.Y.: Prometheus Books.

Proctor, George. N.d. *Proctor's History of the Crusades.* Philadelphia: John E. Potter and Company.

Ralls, Karen. 2004. The Grail: A quest for our times. *Phenomena* (January–February), 47–51.

Ravenscroft, Trevor. 1982. *The Spear of Destiny.* Boston: Weiser Books.

Regolo, Luciano. 1995. Sindon, a mystery called woman. *Chi* (August). Abridged in Guscin 1998, 59–60.

Relics in the Christian faith. 2005. http://www.greeleynet.com/~maxalla/ OKHSSub/ChristianRelicRescue.html. Accessed February 28.

Rhein, Reginald W., Jr. 1980. The Shroud of Turin: Medical examiners disagree. *Medical World News* 21, 6 (December 22), 40–50.

Rogers, Raymond N. 2004. Shroud not hoax, not miracle. Letter to the editor, *Skeptical Inquirer* 28, 4 (July–August), 69.

———. 2005a. Rebuttal to Joe Nickell. *Skeptical Inquirer* 29, 3 (May–June), 16–17.

———. 2005b. Studies on the radiocarbon sample from the Shroud of Turin. *Thermochimica Acta* 425, 189–94.

Rogo, D. Scott. 1982. *Miracles: A Parascientific Inquiry into Wondrous Phenomena.* New York: Dial Press.

Rosenfeld, Ammon, and Shimon Ilani. 2002. Letter to the editor, *Biblical Archaeology Review* (September 17). Reproduced in Lemaire 2002.

Royal Ontario Museum. 2002. James ossuary display text, exhibit of November 15–December 29.

Rufinus. [ca. 402]. *Church History.* Quoted in translation in Thiede and d'Ancona 2002, 20–22.

Ryan, Terri Jo. 2002. Baylor religion professors anxious to check out "James" bone box. *Tribune-Herald* (Waco, Tex.), November 4.

Samuels, David. 2004. Written in stone. *New Yorker* (April 12), 48–59.

Santuario Del Volto Santo. 2005. Historical short essay on Manoppello. http://www.Voltosanto.it/english/the_story/the_story.htm. Accessed July 19.

Sava, Dr. Anthony. 1977. In *Proceedings on the 1977 United States Conference of Research on the Shroud Turin.* Bronx, N.Y.: Holy Shroud Guild.

Scavone, Daniel C. 1989. *The Shroud of Turin.* Great Mysteries series. San Diego, Calif.: Greenhaven Press.

Schafersman, Steven D. 1982. Science, the public and the Shroud of Turin. *Skeptical Inquirer* 6, 3 (spring), 37–56.

Schwalbe, L. A., and R. N. Rogers. 1982. Physics and chemistry of the Shroud of Turin: A summary of the 1978 investigation. *Analytica Chimica Acta* 135, 3–49.

Scrivener, Leslie. 2002. Expert skeptical about ossuary. *Toronto Star,* November 25.

Secrets of the Da Vinci Code. 2004. Collector's edition. *U.S. News and World Report.*

Shuman, Ellis. 2002. "Brother of Jesus" bone-box plot thickens. http://web.israelinsider.com . . . , November 5.

Smith, Morton. 1973. *The Secret Gospel.* New York: Harper and Row.

Sox, David. 1978. *File on the Shroud.* London: Coronet Books.

———. 1987. *Unmasking the Forger: The Dossena Deception.* London: Unwin Hyman.

Spear of Jesus. 2004. TV documentary, Discovery Channel, March 17.

Stravinskas, M. J. 2002. *Catholic Dictionary.* Huntington, Ind.: Our Sunday Visitor.

Thiede, Carsten Peter, and Matthew d'Ancona. 2002. *The Quest for the True Cross.* New York: Palgrave.

Tuchman, Barbara W. 1978. *A Distant Mirror: The Calamitous 14th Century.* New York: Ballantine Books.

Twain, Mark. 1869. *The Innocents Abroad.* Reprint, New York: Modern Library, 2003.

Ubelaker, Douglas, and Henry Scammell. 1992. *Bones: A Forensic Detective's Casebook.* New York: HarperCollins.

Van Biema, David. 1998. Science and the shroud. *Time* (April 20), 53–61.

———. 2002. The brother of Jesus? *Time.* www.time.com/time/magazine/printout/ . . . , October 27.

Walsh, John. 1963. *The Shroud.* New York: Random House.

Walsh, John Evangelist. 1985. *The Bones of St. Peter.* Garden City, N.Y.: Image Books.

Ward, Kaari, ed. 1987. *Jesus and His Times.* Pleasantville, N.Y.: Reader's Digest Association.

Whanger, Mary, and Alan Whanger. 1998. *The Shroud of Turin: An Adventure of Discovery.* Franklin, Tenn.: Providence House.

Wilcox, Robert K. 1977. *Shroud.* New York: Macmillan.

Wilford, John Noble. 2002. Experts question authenticity of bone box of "brother of Jesus." *New York Times,* December 3.

Wilson, Ian. 1979. *The Shroud of Turin,* rev. ed. Garden City, N.Y.: Image Books.

————. 1998. *The Blood and the Shroud.* New York: Free Press.

Wong, Margaret. 2004. Hong Kong critics belittle China's loan of Buddha's relic. *Arizona Daily Star,* May 26.

Woodward, Kenneth L. 1990. *Making Saints: How the Catholic Church Determines Who Becomes a Saint, Who Doesn't, and Why.* New York: Simon and Schuster.

Wuenschel, Edward A. 1957. *Self-Portrait of Christ: The Holy Shroud of Turin.* Esopus, N.Y.: Holy Shroud Guild.

Index